Multi-Million Dollar Private Practice

Multi-Million Dollar PRIVATE PRACTICE

*How to Build a Mental Health Private Practice that
Creates a Massive Impact, Supports Your Dreams,
and Generates Millions of Dollars
Consistently Every Single Year*

Soribel Martinez

LCSW, MBA

NEW YORK

LONDON • NASHVILLE • MELBOURNE • VANCOUVER

Multi-Million Dollar PRIVATE PRACTICE

How to Build a Mental Health Private Practice That Creates a Massive Impact, Supports Your Dreams, and Generates Millions of Dollars Consistently Every Single Year

Published in New York, New York, by Morgan James Publishing. Morgan James is a trademark of Morgan James, LLC. www.MorganJamesPublishing.com

Proudly distributed by Publishers Group West®

Morgan James BOGO™

A **FREE** ebook edition is available for you or a friend with the purchase of this print book.

_____

CLEARLY SIGN YOUR NAME ABOVE

Instructions to claim your free ebook edition:
1. Visit MorganJamesBOGO.com
2. Sign your name CLEARLY in the space above
3. Complete the form and submit a photo of this entire page
4. You or your friend can download the ebook to your preferred device

ISBN 9781636982762 paperback
ISBN 9781636982779 ebook
Library of Congress Control Number: 2023942913

Cover Design by:
Rachel Lopez
www.r2cdesign.com

Interior Design by:
Chris Treccani
www.3dogcreative.net

Morgan James is a proud partner of Habitat for Humanity Peninsula and Greater Williamsburg. Partners in building since 2006.

Get involved today! Visit: www.morgan-james-publishing.com/giving-back

Dedicated to every single woman in the world who has decided to build her queendom legacy despite the struggles, challenges and adversity she has faced. To every woman who has chosen to care for her offspring and leave them a legacy of change and transformation that they can pass on to the future generations.

To every single mother who has not allowed the social stigma and unrealistic expectations to stop them from creating the life and business of their dreams so they can provide the best life, opportunities and possibilities for their children

To every woman who has decided to show up unapologetically because, in all reality, there is no one to apologize to.

To every woman who has discovered her uniqueness, gifts, and ability and has created a way to break generational trauma, curses and limitations to build a multi-million-dollar brand, despite where they come from.

To every woman before me who has paved the path to help me be here today. The women of the path who paid the price so my future can be bright and abundant. To every woman of the past who made her dreams, hopes, and ambitions come into a reality. I honor you today, as I pave the future of the woman who is coming after me.

To my son John-Anthony, the biggest reason why I am here today. The reason I decided after two brain aneurysms and surgery, to do all that was in my power to be here. I am honored to see you grow to be the man you were created to be. The man who will also change the lives of millions in your prospective career or path of choice. I love you.

Table of Contents

Acknowledgments

John Anthony, thank you for being my son and allowing me to guide your path to a bright future. I love you and hope that I am the hero you need to look up to every day when things may not be working out for you. Remember that you are an unbreakable man with an unbreakable purpose, vision, and mission in the world. I trust that you will find it soon. Love you.

Every Queen and every King that has been part of my Queendom legacy journey who supported me and helped make this book a reality.

I want to thank every woman who picks up this book, gets inspired and motivated, and decides she is good enough to build her queendom legacy. Thank you to every woman who decides she doesn't have to apologize for how she shows up for herself, for her community, and for the world.

Introduction

I always knew writing books was part of my purpose and the reason God created me. I once prayed that God would give me experiences worth writing about. As a young child, I didn't know the depths of what I manifested with that prayer, but what I've learned as I write is that each book begins to take shape long before its writer puts pen to paper or fingers to a keyboard. This particular book began in 2018.

This book is in your hands because I refused to let go of those dreams.

When my parents moved to the United States and left me in the care of an abusive aunt in the Dominican Republic, I held on.

Sitting in the Pentecostal church and hearing that money was the root of all evil, I held onto a dream which allowed me to question that message.

Hearing messages from the church that school and education were a path toward hell, I decided my desire for education was more powerful than my fear.

When a language barrier almost caused me to fail out of college, I looked for support, put in the hours, and chased a dream.

When I quit medical school because it didn't fit my life, I knew I was destined to help others and trusted I would find a way to do just that.

When fertility struggles and my yearning for motherhood broke my heart, I held onto the dream of being both a successful business owner and a mother.

When two brain aneurysms and a dangerous operation threatened my life, I recommitted to my purpose and found a way.

I didn't give up on those dreams. I held them in a clenched fist through every obstacle. But all that adversity has a way of making your dreams a bit murky—as though you're gazing at your future through muddy water. After brain surgery, I knew I needed to reconnect with my purpose. I needed clarity. Clarity requires us to get quiet, to listen to our Creator, and then take massive, inspired action toward our goals.

None of the things I experienced were big enough to stop me because my purpose was given to me by my Creator. Nothing you've had to overcome is powerful enough to pull you away from your purpose, either.

In 2018, I was a school social worker providing services to students in a bilingual school who needed it. I was having a positive impact on the Latinx community and finding success. But I had bigger dreams than that position could help me accomplish.

My dreams were multifaceted. I wanted to provide a lifestyle that would allow my son to flourish. I wanted to offer him a private education, music lessons, and anything to help him fulfill whatever dreams his tiny heart held. As I watched him one summer afternoon, playing on the floor while I was holding a bill for his school tuition I couldn't afford to pay, I knew I needed to do more.

In addition to providing a better life for my family, I wanted to have a larger impact on the world. Working in schools allowed me to impact the lives of many youngsters. Still, I was limited by the confines of a school schedule, the realities of an enormous caseload, and the bureaucracy of the educational system.

I started writing this book the day I decided to register for my licensing exam and begin working in private practice. I started writing this book when I realized the courses I took in my undergraduate and graduate degree programs prepared me for providing therapy and enriching others' lives but did not prepare me for running a business. Even the courses I took as an MBA student didn't prepare me for the realities of starting and running a heart-centered, purpose-driven business. See, my business is as concerned with impact as it is with profits. I want to help as many people as possible to live the lives they want, but I also want to send my kid to private school and drive a Mercedes convertible while I do it. Massive impact, massive profit—that's the business I teach in this book and in my courses, coaching, and mentorship programs.

This book is one part dreams, one part mindset, and one part strategy. I will remind you that building a business is about dreaming and about cultivating a mindset that allows you to hold on to those dreams no matter what adversities life throws your way. Then, I'll teach you the Multi-Million Dollar Private Practice Framework™, an eight-part system I created as I built my therapy practice from a solo practice, I operated part-time into a thriving group practice serving thousands of clients and employing more than 30 people.

I started writing this book when I decided to start a private practice, but I wasn't ready to publish it and to give it to you until I'd reached a level of success that past me only dreamed of.

I wrote this book because, just like me, there are thousands and thousands of women wanting to open a private practice with big dreams, big desires, and a drive to impact the community, but things are standing in their way. Grief, loss, trauma, financial strain, divorce, single parenthood, a focus on caring for others, limiting beliefs, and many other issues, problems, or ideas. Sometimes these obstacles are so enormous we can't see around them to get back to the path of our dreams.

This book will help you break down the roadblocks. This allows you to heal first and use that healing as a catalyst for returning to your dreams and desires. We will systematically dismantle the roadblocks you can't see around and move the smaller ones out of the way. We will turn this windy, rutted path into a paved expressway of confidence, empowerment, and a drive to fulfill your desires, your purpose.

Once we've done all the inner work to heal and reconnect, I will give you tools and strategies so you can work on all the possibilities you imagined for yourself when you started working in the mental health field. Everything is possible for you. I wrote this book to show you how.

I created the Multi-Million Dollar Private Practice Framework™ because when I started in private practice, I didn't have a mentor I could look up to who was doing the work I wanted to do, having the impact I wanted to have, and living the lifestyle I wanted to live. When you can't find what you need, you create it. I made a framework that allowed me to reach the success I wanted. These pillars became my roadmap, my to do list, and my step-by-step process for growth and expansion in my business. Every time I make a decision in my business, I go back to the framework because if I continue to build my business in the same manner I built the foundation, everything I do is in alignment. Alignment is where we thrive.

This framework will work for you, too. The MMDPP Framework™ is the path to fulfilling the purpose, vision, and mission of your business. It's the path toward the lifestyle you want to live. It's also the path toward the dreams of a young girl in the Dominican Republic who built a Queendom and continues to expand her legacy. Before you start reading, I invite you to email me. Tell me what dream you hope to fulfill with the framework outlined in this book. What goals do you have? What purpose are you committed to reconnecting to? I really mean it; email me at soribel@soribelmartinez.com. I will reply personally if you grant me the honor of sharing your dream.

EMAIL SORIBEL

This book is a guide for you as you build and grow your private practice. Write in the margins, dog-ear pages you want to return to, and don't let it sit on your shelf too long. As you scale your business, you'll want to refer back to the contents of each chapter again and again. Part 1 will help when you feel disconnected from your purpose and unsure if you're on the right path. Part 2 will help you explore why starting your private practice is the right move for both your own financial gain and the impact you want to have in the world. Part 3 contains the Multi-Million Dollar Private Practice Framework™, a proven system many mental health practitioners use to build the life and business of their dreams.

Now, let's get into the business of building your dream business.

Part 1

Mindset and Alignment

"Ninety to ninety-five percent of your business is spiritual, the rest is strategies. Don't neglect the spiritual component."
~Soribel Martinez, LCSW

I tell every business coaching client, and any person sitting in the audience at one of my speaking events, that most of their business success is spiritual. People either nod or raise a skeptical eyebrow. But by the time I finish discussing the things I'll share with you in the first part of this book, they're all nodding along with me the next time I say it.

You cannot ignore your spiritual self and do well in business. Sure, you might make some money, but you won't have the impact you want to have. You won't have the satisfaction you crave, and you'll wind up exhausted, overworked, burned out, and done. You might even lose the business entirely.

I don't want that path for you. I want you to have a business that lights you up, fills you with energy, and leads you toward your purpose-driven goals.

Chapter 1

Manifest Your Deepest Desires

Birdsong and chirping sounds of insects formed the soundtrack of my dreams. At seven years old, I lay on the ground under a Dominican sky, my long legs stretched out and crossed at the ankles. To any observer, I was counting stars and watching for a celestial event like a comet flying by. But in my mind, I was decades away and dreaming of the life I wanted to live. As a young girl, unrestrained by societal constructs, limiting ideas, and confidence-stripping belief systems, I was free to dream big. And I did.

I dreamed of starting out in life like my Papi, a business executive who managed an agricultural bank and wore freshly pressed suits to work each day. But my dreams weren't just written in those stars; they stretched further. I wouldn't manage a company run by someone else. I'd own one. I'd create a business that would help people, that would change the world for the better.

As more stars filled the sky, I felt God calling me for more. I dreamed of writing books that could change lives, and of passing on my knowledge, my ability to dream, and my desire for a better world for future generations. At seven, I couldn't know the exact shape these dreams would take, but, in my innocence, I was fully able to connect to my Creator and understand that I was meant to build an empire of a new sort, one focused on enriching lives instead of lining pockets.

As children, we are connected to our deepest desires. We are born with these desires because God created us with a purpose. The desires we have as young children are the desires God gives us to reach our potential. As children, we are called to follow those desires and build our dreams. We have no limitations; we believe everything is possible. As we grow, we encounter societal expectations and other forces that fill our brains with limiting messages telling us the things we dream of aren't possible. Society teaches us what we can't have and pulls us away from our dreams and desires. Society pulls us away from our purpose.

Sometimes I'd dare to say my dreams aloud, and when I told them to Papi in our cozy kitchen over a shared plate of Dominican food after his workday, he received them with a smile in his eyes.

"Mija, I don't care what career path you choose, you can be a businesswoman, a doctor, an attorney, a teacher, and you may even choose to work for the garbage company and want to be a garbage picker, but one thing I demand from you is that whatever you choose to do, be the best you can be. So if you clean the streets, be the best at cleaning them," he'd encourage with a tap on my nose as punctuation.

Sometimes, though, my young lips made the mistake of sharing my dreams with someone unable to understand them. During family parties, one of my aunts would inevitably tell me I'd be a wonderful wife and mother someday because of some female-approved way I played or cared for others.

"No, I'm going to be a wonderful business owner," I'd reply with my hands on my hips and my braids bouncing along with my attitude.

"Oh, Sori," they'd reply, "you always have something to say, don't you?"

These unsafe dream-catchers couldn't see my dreams and encourage them because they'd forgotten how to dream for themselves. They'd heard and seen the message that a "good Dominican woman" was a doting wife, an agreeable companion, and an overworked mother. Comments about my lofty dreams and strong ideas became commonplace. I heard their snickers and comments and immediately dismissed them. I wasn't angry. I understood, even at that young age, that they hadn't been allowed to dream. I wasn't going to stop. I had the stars, the night air, and Papi's words in my ears. I had everything I needed to be successful inside of me.

Years passed, and I lost Papi, and much of my innocence, to immigration. I was a left-behind child and struggled to regain my footing after arriving in the United States many years after he left. The religious messages preached in Mami's new church only buried my dreams further.

After Papi left for the United States, Mami, left in the Dominican Republic with three children, craved community. She was a spiritual woman, and the Pentecostal Church seemed a remedy for her loneliness and the troubles in her life. Unfortunately, as a young girl with big dreams, the church she chose for our family caused a level of cognitive dissonance I'd struggle with for years to come.

Suddenly, my after-school playtime was replaced by going door to door to preach about God's message. Evening church services overtook the time for homework and the volleyball team I loved. My education was always a priority before Papi left. Once we joined the church, however, the late services spent in a stuffy church, where women wearing long sleeves and even longer skirts batted fans at themselves in a vain attempt at dispelling the steamy Dominican heat, took over.

The experience of giving up the things I loved to receive messages about sin and what God's will was for us caused me to question everything I thought I knew. Papi said education was the most important thing for my brothers and me. He and his siblings were all college-educated thanks to the hard work of my abuela, and the move to the United States was meant to provide us with better opportunities for college and a career. At church, though, the "leaders" called educated people sinners and said that desiring knowledge was going against God's will. I listened to these sermons and responded with the required "Amen" and "Yes, Lord," at appropriate times, but I couldn't shake the feeling that something was amiss.

I wanted to be educated. I wanted to be successful. I wanted to make money and live a life that brought me joy and allowed me to improve the lives of others. I wanted all of that, and I needed education to get it. Did that mean I was sinful? Was I going against God's will for me? Was God's desire for my life out of alignment with my desires? Was my will intrinsically wicked?

I wrestled with this cognitive dissonance for a decade. Our move to the United States brought a new church with the same rules and ideas. Luckily, at that point, I had Papi back, and his words encouraged me to continue prioritizing my education, even though I'd hear the opposite at every church service. I wasn't giving up my dreams, and I wasn't losing focus, but I did start to believe my desires were wrong. I developed limiting beliefs about education, wealth, prosperity, and success that followed me for decades. Those ideas were so ingrained in my psyche that I nearly forgot what my desires were. But I couldn't stay stuck in that place of confusion. I knew what I wanted. I knew what I always dreamed of, and I felt called to move in that direction.

Somewhere in my late teens, as I entered college with a full scholarship, I decided to stop dealing with the cognitive dissonance. I decided to divorce the church and reclaim my power, reconnect to my desires, and give myself the life I wanted. I divorced the pastors, the "leaders," the ideas, and even the parking lot everyone gathered in after services. I decided that seven-year-old Soribel, who felt connected to God and herself, was the real me. I found my purpose again and learned to embrace my desires. I wanted education, I wanted financial success, I wanted joy, and I was going to get all three. Now, I want to urge you to do the same.

Let's undo the societal conditioning around what you can be, have, and do. This is your life, and God gave you a purpose and dreams. Let's make a clear statement about what you actually want out of life. You only get to do this journey once, it's time to stop waiting, and start creating.

The first part of success is to identify what you want. Don't try to respond to that just yet. I don't want the answer that you filter through society's expectations for what you should be, do, or have. That answer won't serve you. The desire I want you to focus on as you read this book and build your business is the one that's inside you. Maybe it's quiet now after years of hiding from society and a lack of belief. Maybe you can't even hear it. That's okay. I'll guide you to reconnect with that little voice that knows who you are and what you're meant to do on this Earth.

For now, I want you to think about the following.

What did you want to be before society told you it was impossible?

What life did you imagine for yourself before the stress of life made you stop dreaming?

What if those dreams and that longing signified the truest version of yourself?

Reclaiming my power from limiting beliefs about success, money, and joy required that I get rid of the shackles of religious shame and reconnect to God's true form. My God is not vindictive. He does not punish people who desire education or success. He doesn't curse women for cutting their hair, wearing skirts above the ankle, or putting on mascara. Reclaiming my power required me to find the God I knew at seven, the one who whispered to me as I lay on the ground, soiling the clothes Mami rolled her eyes at when she had to wash them. Once I reconnected with my true Creator, I learned that my desires were God's desires for me.

Once you connect with your Creator and identify your true purpose in this world, you can dream again. Once you can dream, you're ready to create a vision and a mission that aligns with your purpose. Let's dive into the Million-Dollar Alignment Framework.

MILLION-DOLLAR ALIGNMENT FRAMEWORK

PURPOSE
This is why you are here. It's the reason God created you — **your motivation.**

VISION
This is what you are meant to do and what impact you want to have on the world.

MISSION
This is how you fulfill your purpose and vision. It's the tiny steps along the path to your vision.

PURPOSE

Your purpose is why you are here—it's the reason God created you, your motivation. Everything God creates has a purpose. The purpose of the honeybee is to pollinate flowers and spread life across the globe. The purpose of the trees is to change carbon dioxide into life-giving air, keep our soil rooted in place, and provide shade to the living things that require protection from the sun.

Your purpose was inside you the day God designed you. You don't need instructions from the latest TikTok video, your great Aunt Edna, or even from the pastor at your church. You only need to get quiet enough to connect to your Source, hear the whisper of encouragement, and feel the nudge toward your next right thing.

Your purpose aligns with your values—what you believe to be true about yourself and about how you fit into the world. Maybe you value family and education above all else. Perhaps your most important values are creativity and freedom. Your purpose will align with whatever you hold dear because your desires and soul were formed together.

VISION

Your vision is what you're meant to do and what impact you want to have on the world. Perhaps your vision is helping others heal or caring for children in need. Maybe you aspire to connect people, or to create a more beautiful world. Your vision is the end of a blueprint or road map to help you construct your dreams. We lose the map and get lost when we take steps that aren't aligned with our purpose. When we do what others want or expect us to do or seek external validation for our actions, we detour from our path, and that's okay. We don't need to spend time beating ourselves up for those detours now. We made them, and we accept them as part of our path. Now, though, you're only taking steps that align with your purpose.

Whenever you make a decision in life or business, I want you to run it through your alignment filter. Does hiring an assistant for your business allow you to fulfill your purpose in greater ways? Does it free up your energy for more impactful action while also improving the lives of the person you hire? If so, then what are you waiting for? Does buying a house that adequately shelters those you love fit within your purpose of creating a joyful life? Is your purpose to make the world beautiful with your art or to connect people through words?

MISSION

Your mission is how you fulfill your purpose and vision. It's the tiny steps along the path to your vision. A mission is the nitty-gritty of how you will do life and business. Will you be a doctor, an inventor, a teacher, or an astronaut? Will you write books, create art, or make others laugh? What action steps will you take to fulfill your purpose and vision?

Your mission is a plan, and it's open to modifications as you grow and learn. Like me, you may start helping others heal by being a therapist, but then realize you can increase your impact (and achieve your vision on a greater scale) by running a group practice capable of serving thousands of people.

Your purpose, vision, and mission are important because they guide every decision you will make about life and business as you read this book and in the years to come. Your vision and mission keep you focused on your purpose and the path God set before you. When you have alignment in your purpose, vision, and mission, you will find it easy to embrace and communicate your deepest desires.

Once you find alignment, no force will have the power to take away your voice or cause you to believe a story about what you can have, be, and do. Alignment reinforces your commitment to living your true purpose and embracing the greatness designed for you.

> How do we find alignment?

I lay out these steps in more detail in the companion manual for my Multi-Million-Dollar Private Practice coaching and mentorship programs, but here is an overview.

STEP 1: SELF-EVALUATION

Complete a self-evaluation to understand where you are and how you got there.

How satisfied are you with your life right now? Think about your satisfaction at home, in relationships, and in your career.

How did you arrive at that level of satisfaction? What experiences, pressures, and learning caused you to settle at that level?

For this step, I had to figure out what disconnected me from the dreams I carried as a young girl. It wasn't one thing for me, and it likely isn't for you either. In my situation, it was trauma caused by immigration, decades of social conditioning, and strict religious teachings. Perhaps you were derailed by something similar, or maybe you found yourself surrounded by people telling you what you couldn't do instead of what you could. Dig deep and figure out why you wound up where you are now. There's always a reason.

STEP 2: HEALING

Once we understand where we're at, we have to heal. Healing looks different for each of us, but it has the same goals: shifting your mindset, transforming limiting beliefs, and believing that you deserve what you want out of life.

I had to heal religious trauma and learn to live a spiritual life that didn't require attending church to connect with God. God is not in church. I had to learn that God is inside me and every one of us all the time because He created us to do great work on Earth. Maybe you need to heal from trauma caused by your parents or shame over past mistakes.

Here are my strategies for healing:

- Reading personal development books helps recondition and reprogram your mind with new information that aligns with your purpose and desires.
- Seeking therapy to heal past trauma, work through limiting beliefs, and learn to put your needs first. Taking care of yourself is not selfish. When you run a business, it reflects

you, and the success of everyone your business touches, from employees to clients, depends on your health.

- Start talking to people doing the sort of work you want to do in the world. I had a professor in college who became the first person to serve this purpose in my life. Since then, I've hired mentors and business coaches and attended conferences where people doing great healing work collaborate and learn together.

- Reprogram your beliefs about self-care. I believe that a successful business owner needs a holistic self-care practice. This isn't trips to the nail salon or face masks, although those things may be a part of it. Holistic self-care is caring for your mind, body, and soul daily, weekly, monthly, and yearly. For me, this means daily journaling, meditating, and praying. I also ensure I get adequate sleep and move my body in joyful ways. I read, learn, and study to improve my mind and build more of the life I love. I connect with the people I love and make sure to protect that time.

- Reframe self-criticism into affirmations. We all have negative thoughts from time to time, but when you aren't chasing your dreams, it's a pretty good bet your self-talk is pretty negative. If you catch yourself saying things such as "Who am I to think I can run a business?" or "I'm too _____ to be a successful business owner," it's time to learn to stop those negative thoughts in their tracks. The easiest way to do this is to stop any time you have one and reframe it into a positive affirmation. Instead of "I'll never be able to get enough clients to support my business," try "I am open to receiving as many clients as I need to support my growing business." I talk more about managing thoughts and how they impact behavior in Chapter 3.

STEP 3: IDENTIFY WHAT YOU *REALLY* WANT—YOUR DESIRES ARE FROM THE DIVINE

When you've spent your life forming your desires around what your parents, friends, and society say you should want, you lose track of your true desires. Perhaps, like me, your conditioning caused you to believe your desires are inherently wrong or sinful. Now that you've taken steps to heal those parts of you, you realize that God puts desires in your heart because they will guide you closer to fulfilling your purpose. Now, you're ready to tell the world what you really want.

This part of the process requires you to get quiet, look internally, and block out all the noise telling you what you are allowed to be, do, or have. Imagine there are no constraints. Do you want a Villa in Italy? A yacht parked in the Florida Keys? Write it down. Do you want to create a nonprofit that helps people battling cancer or supports families who've lost a child? Write it down. Do you want to build a business? What kind? How much money do you want your business to make each year? How many people do you want to offer employment opportunities to? What sort of employer do you want to be? Write it all down.

You get to have everything you want in life, and God will support you along your journey. The only requirement is to stay connected to your purpose and continuously do your part. It won't be easy, but I promise you, it will be worth it.

STEP 4: CREATE GOALS AND AN ACTION PLAN IN ALIGNMENT WITH YOUR PURPOSE

Once you've started your healing work (yes, started…we're never really finished, so you'll probably revisit step 2 over and over again) and written down your actual desires, you're ready to create goals and a plan that support your purpose, vision, and mission.

It's one thing to want to start a nonprofit or buy a yacht, but a desire without a plan is a wish, and I've never known a wish to come true without some sort of action.

Your goals must align with your purpose, vision, and mission. Early in my journey, my goal was to attend medical school and become a doctor. As I learned more about myself and our world, my goal changed. The same will be true for you.

Your goals must be as big as your vision. Alignment is only one part of the whole picture; your dreams should be big enough to scare you a bit.

Your goals will determine your action plan. When my goals changed, my plan did as well. Your plan will change as you learn and grow. Be open to that change and be willing to adjust as you learn more about yourself and your purpose.

Part of your plan should be to find a support system. This will likely include friends and family, but you'll also want mentors, business coaches, and other people who are building the sort of business you are. As part of my plan, I also vowed to limit interactions with people who discouraged me from moving to the next level, something I still do today. I connected with professors who inspired me and, later, with people doing the sort of work I wanted to do in the world.

CHAPTER TAKEAWAYS

- Your purpose is the reason you were created and the work that you will do in the world to impact other people.
- Your purpose guides you to be an active contributor to the world and leave it better than you found it.
- Your purpose must guide all of your decision-making.

- Personal healing is in the forefront of your success in life and business because you are your business, and you are your brand. The level of healing, awareness, and transformation in your personal life affects your business success.
- Your goals are driven by your vision and your mission. Your goals should be as big as your vision. They should make you feel a bit scared.
- A goal without a plan is just a dream. You need a step-by-step roadmap to get you from where you are now to where you want to be.

Chapter 2

Cultivate a Leadership Mindset

The early summer sunlight reflected off the hardwood floor where John Anthony played with his cars and trucks. His head was bent in concentration, and his legs folded in a way only a tiny child could manage. He looked at me and smiled.

"Mami, look what I made." He held his creation in his little-boy fingers.

"Tell me about it," I encouraged, opening my arms and inviting him into my embrace.

His words flowed over me, but none of them really stuck. I was miles away on a train of anxiety and fear. I'd been sitting at the dining room table for hours trying to figure out how I could continue to afford the life I had built for my boy and me. When I made the decision to become a single mother, I made it knowing the difficulties I faced, but confident I could manage them.

I took a job at a school district so my hours matched my boy's. I had benefits and a salary and summers off to watch him grow. But, the truth was that I struggled. I couldn't see a way to continue paying for John Anthony's private school tuition.

Some people might tell me to pull him out of private school and save the money, but that was never an option I considered. I believe in private school, and I wanted John Anthony to have all the opportunities and connections a private school education would afford him. No, I wasn't putting him in the public schools where we lived. I needed to woman up and find a way to make this life work.

John Anthony returned to his play, and I turned my attention back to the bills and financial documents in front of me. I closed my eyes and took a breath. I prayed the prayer that got me through college, graduate school, and the early days of my career.

"God, show me the path. I am willing to do my part. Put the people and resources I need in my path so I can make things happen."

Then I heard the whisper. It was so faint I'd have missed it if the heat of the day caused the air conditioning to click on at that moment.

"You're sitting on gold."

I kept my eyes closed, recognizing the voice of my creator, the voice that answered my prayers since I was seven. Sounds of John Anthony's toys faded into background noise, and I could hear the ticking of my kitchen clock.

"You're sitting on gold. Get your license and go into business."

"Holy moly alligators! YES!" I shouted so loud that John Anthony glanced my way. I smiled at him, assuring him that his mother was not crazy, just inspired.

I stood, grabbed my laptop from my bedroom, and got down to the business of starting a business.

Running my own business was always my goal, as you read in chapter one, but I kept putting it off. I wanted to wait until John Anthony was older before I dedicated that sort of time to my professional life. I had a million reasons why I hadn't started. Now, I realized that my son was not a reason I couldn't start my own business. He was the reason I needed to.

I had massive dreams for myself and for my boy. I wanted to create a legacy he could pass down to future generations of hard work, creativity, inspired action, and helping our world become a better place. If I wanted to build that legacy for him, I needed to get to work.

Now, I had a new goal: Get my license so I could start a private therapy practice. Next, I needed a plan, a roadmap to get me to my goal and help me fulfill my purpose on Earth in new ways.

At that moment, I needed to ignite my leadership mindset. I needed to stop waiting for my problems to fix themselves, and start behaving like the unbreakable woman I am. I shared my plan with my friend, Dex, who always believed in me, my dreams, and my vision. He gave me the money to register for the exam. I registered for a test six weeks away. I found an online training preparation program and then I hit my first roadblock. I didn't even have enough money to pay for the course I needed to take to prepare myself for the licensing exam.

But, we cannot let a little thing like our bank account balance dictate our success. So, I reached out to the creator of the course and asked for a payment plan. The organization said yes immediately, and I created a study plan. I would glue myself to my chair from morning until night because I knew that with the language barrier I would need to study harder than my peers. I would break for meals and sleep and then be back in that chair again.

I asked for help from my family to care for John Anthony. Sure, I would miss him, and I could have let guilt come in and tell me I wasn't being a good mother—that I was ignoring my son in order to take care of myself. But I couldn't do that to John Anthony. He deserves a mom who is fulfilled and who can take care of him and provide everything he needs. I was on a quest to be that person.

If you're starting to dream again after reading chapter one of this book, and you know what you want, it's time to take the first step toward getting it. You can build the multi-million-dollar private practice of your dreams as long as you have a leadership mindset.

Everyone is born a leader, but not all people become leaders. We are born with the potential for greatness as long as we work to cultivate it. Some people develop leadership qualities and some don't. Today and every day afterward, you are someone who develops your leadership skills. Starting today, you will implement these principles of leadership in your life so that your business thrives.

The principles of a Multi-Million-Dollar Leadership Mindset Framework™ include:

- Personal leadership
- Aligned communication
- Decision-making
- More passion, less perfection
- Influence, not control
- Change initiation

MULTI-MILLION DOLLAR BUSINESS MINDSET FORMULA™

PURPOSE, VISION, MISSION

INSPIRATION

STRATEGY

THE PRINCIPLES OF A MULTI-MILLION DOLLAR LEADERSHIP MINDSET

* Personal Leadership
* Aligned Communication
* Decision Making
* More Passion, Less Perfection
* Influence, Not Control
* Change Initiation

ACTIONS

Let's dive into how you will cultivate your leadership mindset.

PERSONAL LEADERSHIP

A leader takes responsibility for their own actions and destiny. Be the captain of your own ship and take steps to develop yourself. Becoming a leader requires you to identify your knowledge gaps and take steps to learn what you don't know without someone managing you. You must manage yourself.

Managing me, at first, involved putting everything else aside and studying like my life depended on it—in some ways it did.

That same strategy I used to study for my licensing exam works when I need to learn more about business, when I decide to add new services, and when I decide to write books.

If you're anything like me when I started my practice, there is a lot you don't know about how to build, run, and scale a successful business. That's fine, as long as you are open to learning and growth. But let's not start with business concepts. Leaders develop in all areas of life. Have you always wished you were the sort of person to make your bed every morning? Start today. Put this book down and go make your bed. Do you always say you wish you exercised more? Get up and go for a walk right now. It's time to do the things you want to do, and become the person you want to become. You have what it takes.

Once you are a leader of yourself, move outward to your loved ones. Show up as a leader at home and with your friends, because you cannot extend to the world what you fail to practice in your personal life. Leaders guide with influence, inspired action, and compassion. Leaders do not rely on fear or manipulation. Are you guilty of yelling at your children to get them to do what you want? You can apologize to them and try to do better. Do you fail to speak up when someone you love hurts you because you fear confrontation? It's time to work that out now because there will be plenty of confrontation to come as you scale your business.

ALIGNED COMMUNICATION

When I was a young girl, I witnessed adults around me smoking while telling kids not to smoke. Then we were all surprised when the child tried a cigarette. I saw children punished for hitting someone else with a swat to their own backside, and then we were surprised that these children never learned that hitting doesn't solve problems. At the time, this troubled me, and I didn't know why. Now, as I sit here, the leader of a multimillion-dollar private practice, the leader of a harmonious (mostly) home, and the leader of my destiny, I know why this bothered me. The adults around me did not have aligned communication.

A leader knows what they want out of life and business and can articulate it. What's more, what they want aligns with their vision, mission, and purpose. A leader's vision must be clear as water. When this is the case, your words and actions make sense to those around you. You have congruence. As a leader, you say what you mean, stick to the things you say, and practice what you ask of others.

I always said I wanted to start a business, and that I wanted to have a massive impact on the world. But I was playing it safe with a salaried job with benefits. Once I aligned my words with how I lived my life, I found an ease and flow that helped me grow my business, and add author, speaker, and business coach to my resume.

DECISION-MAKING

Making a decision to move forward in your business requires three steps. Sitting in the middle of a financial crisis, I knew I needed to do something. As leaders, we are constantly evaluating the next step, seeing possibilities, and problem-solving. Leaders focus on solutions, not the problem. In business, I've found that there are four parts to decision-making that help to build momentum and ensure alignment.

First, I make decisions quickly. I brainstorm possible solutions and then I pick one. Sitting there at my kitchen table, with my bills piled around me, I searched for possibilities: getting a summer job, working part-time for an agency, reducing spending in various areas, and starting my own business. The solution I picked was the one in alignment with my purpose of helping as many people as possible to create the life they were meant to live. Don't get stuck in a spinning web of indecision. You can always change your mind later.

The second part of decision-making I practice is not polling the outside world. Leaders may collaborate with others to brainstorm solutions, but, ultimately, the decision is theirs. For me, looking inward starts with a prayer for guidance. "God, show me the path. I'm willing to do my part. Put the people and resources I need in my path."

Once I decide, I must take inspired action. An inspired action is one small thing you can do to start the momentum toward your goal. My decision to start my own practice led to the inspired action of registering for the test. Once I registered, there was no going back. If you decide to start your business right now, maybe you should create a business email address. Perhaps you register a limited liability company, or create a logo. Pick one thing to start your momentum and motivate you to move forward.

After that first bit of inspired action, I urge leaders to take massive action. Massive action requires planning, preparation, and speed. I like to think of a cheetah on the hunt. She crouches in the grass, watching a herd of antelope. She doesn't move right away. She's plotting, her tail twitching, her eyes intense and focused. She determines which animal is her next meal. She plans her attack, and then she lunges, giving chase. She is relentless. Massive action is vital to decision-making. A decision without action is just a wish.

MORE PASSION, LESS PERFECTION

Throughout college and early in my career, the way I spoke, wrote, and understood English left me feeling inadequate. How could I build a business and ask others to look up to me if I couldn't put nouns and adjectives in the right order in a sentence? Did the pause I took to translate a question into Spanish in my head make me appear stupid or hesitant?

To become a true leader, I needed to stop asking myself for perfection. The truth is that perfection is not available to us. We will always have quirks, like an accent, or a habit of clearing your throat too much. We may have a hair out of place or lipstick on our teeth. Striving for perfection will drain your energy and success out of your business.

Instead of perfection, seek to do things with passion.

- Passion fuels our drive for learning, improvement, and growth.
- Passion creates the desire to be in alignment and alignment fuels momentum, momentum renews passion, this cycle continues.
- Passion spurs authenticity, which is what people connect to—it's why people will hire you and want to work for you.

I still have an accent, I still mix up words, and I still have to take extra time to complete writing tasks in English. But now I view this differently. When someone hears me speak at an event or via one of my online training sessions, they remember me because the way I speak and understand English makes me unique. Other women who are immigrants look at me and know that they can build success as well. The women who seek therapy with my practice know they can receive services in English, Spanish, or Portuguese. Being a Dominican-American immigrant does not hinder my business; it is one reason I'm successful.

INFLUENCE, NOT CONTROL

A leader understands that leadership is not about control, but about influence. Influence is the ability to affect someone's character, growth, or behavior. Then a leader has the influence of bringing others into their vision. So, in order to lead people, you must have a vision worthy of inspiring others. Then you have to live your purpose and mission every day. The blind are not guiding the blind here. People will watch you and join your mission because they believe in your vision and see you living your purpose.

Growing up in the Pentecostal Church, I found myself surrounded by so-called "leaders" who sought to control the congregation because it gave them a sense of power. They controlled what we did, who we could befriend, what we wore, and even how long our hair was. The control of these quasi-leaders damaged my relationship with God and my trust in myself.

Now, as a leader, I seek to change others' lives based on the work I'm doing in the world. I motivate through positivity, modeling the behaviors I want others to adopt, and owning my mistakes.

CHANGE INITIATION

Leaders initiate change and transformation rather than waiting for others to take the lead. The cheetah stalking her prey doesn't wait for others to decide, and she isn't looking left or right for someone to do the hard work for her. She is laser-focused on her objective. She doesn't question her decision once she's made it. Her validation comes from within.

As the leader of my business, I do not wait for my employees to initiate a change in how we serve clients. Nor do I poll my friends or family about what they think I should do. I analyze the business and I decide our next steps. That doesn't mean I don't invite suggestions for improvement and innovation; I absolutely do. But ultimately, the initiation of change within my life, my business, and even the world is my job as a leader.

Five weeks after starting the preparation course for my licensing exam, I walked into the testing room, prepared to sit for six hours. The standard four-hour exam, plus extended time because English is my second language. One hour later, I walked out with a passing grade and a renewed sense of purpose. I was on my way to building a private practice that could support the lifestyle I wanted for my son and me.

Cultivating a leadership mindset is vital to the success of your business. The way we think and perceive ourselves, others around us, and the world is everything. The way we think influences how we feel, and our feelings have a lot of control over our behaviors. The behaviors we repeat create our results. This is why I always say mindset is ninety to ninety-five percent of what we need to create sustainable results.

Often, the biggest obstacle to cultivating a leadership mindset is the thoughts and emotions that lower your energy and keep you stuck. When you feel like you can't do something, or let imposter syndrome hold you back from fulfilling your purpose, you are not operating at a high vibration. When you worry about what others think instead of seeking internal guidance and validation, you will lose momentum. A leadership mindset is an antidote to that loss of energy. A leadership mindset says "I can'" or "I don't know yet, but I can learn." This mindset comes from aligning your mission, vision, and purpose, saying yes to your desires, and embracing the principles of a leadership mindset. Then you're ready to manage your thoughts and emotions.

CHAPTER TAKEAWAYS

- Becoming an unbreakable leader requires you to start with changing yourself.
- You must align your communication with your purpose, vision, and mission.
- You must make decisions quickly and act upon them immediately.
- Operating from a place of passion requires you to let go of perfection.
- Leaders positively influence those around them. They never seek to control others.
- Leaders are change initiators—don't wait for others, trust yourself, and take action.

Chapter 3

Manage Your Thoughts
and Emotions

The psychologist's office wasn't much different from any other therapy office I spent time in. A neutral sofa sat against one wall, and the therapist's chair with a table beside it sat at an angle in case the patient wasn't interested in direct eye contact. I kept my eyes trained on the table and the writing tablet that contained the basic information I provided before she asked the question currently rolling around in my mind.

"Why are you here?" she asked again, steepling her fingers and resting them under her chin.

In my mind, I pictured John Anthony, young and alone, without his mother to guide him. I pictured myself lying sprawled on the ground. Would John Anthony be the one to find me after it happened?

"Because I don't want to die," I whispered, raising my eyes and finally meeting the psychologist's gaze.

She smiled, but just barely, and nodded.

"Tell me a bit about what you're thinking these days since getting that phone call."

I took a breath and decided to let it all out. "My brain floats from one thought to another. I can't seem to control it or stop the spiral. It's like I'm grieving the loss of my life already, and I can't stop thinking about the negative possibilities and all the bad that could happen. I could wake up with a slight headache and then die by lunchtime. It could be so sudden that John Anthony is there, screaming, and I can't comfort him. What if it happens at school, and there is no one to pick him up at the end of the day?"

I knew I was rambling, but she just let me go. I continued spilling those thoughts for several minutes before I paused, grabbed a tissue, and tried in vain to catch the tears streaming down my face.

The psychologist inhaled and leaned forward, locking eyes with me. "Soribel, if all you think about is death, if that's the only possibility you see, then you are going to die. You have to be able to see other possibilities in order to make them a reality."

In that moment, it was as if a part of me was reborn—the part of me that fought through everything life threw at me to that point seemed to come back from vacation, ready to get back to the business of building a life. That psychologist's simple statement about self-efficacy was enough to get me out of my dirty chair.

I ended up in that psychologist's office because I believe in getting support when you need it. After my neurologist told me I had two aneurysms and would need brain surgery if I was to have a chance to survive, I froze. My brain couldn't process the information and form a plan. My mindset changed from positive and forward-moving to a throw-in-the-towel nightmare. I recognized I was slipping into a dark place and sought help. Yes, even therapists need a therapist.

So what is this dirty chair, and how do we wind up in it?

BOUNCE BACK FROM THE DIRTY CHAIR PROCESS

BOUNCE BACK FROM THE DIRTY CHAIR PROCESS

MANAGE YOUR THOUGHTS AND EMOTIONS

* Self-Analysis: What is your dirty chair?
* Decide to get up.
* Elicit a support system.
* Find alignment.
* Invite a new perspective.
* Create goals and take massive action.

We all have dirty chairs sitting in the corners of our minds. Some of us have a couple, and some of us have many. These chairs can be labeled sadness, despair, grief, anger, shame, or imposter syndrome. The chairs are the places your mind tries to sit and get comfortable when life seems too hard. The chairs are often emotions; we get stuck in them because of negative thought spirals.

What we think about expands, grows, and becomes our center and our focus. When we sit in a dirty chair and think thoughts that feed the emotion we experience, the filth around us grows. I never do anything right; I can't believe I said that; I should just stop speaking up; my bosses probably hate me—each thought is a bag full of garbage piled on top of you until you can't see around it, can't move to get off the chair, and forget about all the other parts of your life.

My focus after the diagnosis was on all the bad things that could happen. This caused me anxiety and disempowerment. I gave my power over to the situation and let life happen to me instead of taking decisive action. I sat in that dirty chair until I couldn't see any possibility other than death.

In the Harvard Business Review, Susan David, founder of the Harvard/McLean Institute of Coaching, and Christina Congleton, a leadership and change consultant, discuss the idea of emotional agility. David and Congleton propose that effective leaders are not immune to the negative thought processes that keep others stuck. Instead, those who become effective leaders don't suppress the negative thoughts and corresponding emotions, but approach them as a gentle observer and use mindful, productive strategies for managing them.[1]

If we allow ourselves to remain in a dirty chair with swirling negative thoughts, we will not become the leaders God intended us to be. Your dirty chair affects how you show up in the world, how you show up at home with your loved ones, and how you show up for yourself. Moreover, since your business is a reflection of you, any unresolved negative thoughts or emotions will show up in your business.

Unresolved trauma will show up as avoiding confrontation. Unresolved issues around scarcity will keep you from taking risks. An inability to handle frustration and anger will alienate business partners and employees. You must learn to manage thoughts and

---

1   David, S. and Congleton, C., Harvard Business Review (2013, November 1). *Emotional Agility*. Retrieved February 27, 2023, from https://hbr.org/2013/11/emotional-agility

emotions in order to stay at a high vibration and create the success you crave.

Initially, my diagnosis pushed me back into a dirty chair of overwhelm, sadness, uncertainty, and grief. I isolated myself; I didn't even respond to the doctor's office. I didn't move forward with a treatment plan.

So how do we pull ourselves out of the dirty chair? What do we do once we're standing? How do we move forward when our thoughts and emotions threaten to overwhelm us? Here's the dirty chair process.

SELF-ANALYSIS: WHAT IS YOUR DIRTY CHAIR?

First, you must identify what your dirty chair is. We all have at least one, and you may have several. Let's work with one at a time. The dirty chair is made of an experience, the thoughts you have about that experience, and the emotions you feel. This experience/thought/emotion cycle keeps you stuck, disconnects you from your purpose, and results in dissatisfaction with one or more areas of your life. Pay attention to your thought patterns to figure out when you get stuck. Do you get stuck in indecision when you know you need to make a change in your business? Do you relay mistakes you made or things you said and call yourself stupid? Pay attention to the thoughts that repeat, especially if you call yourself names like lazy, incompetent, etc.

Sometimes your dirty chair is the way you view and think about others. Do you constantly tell yourself that your spouse doesn't support you? What stories are you telling yourself about coworkers, employees, or family members? We must figure out what thoughts put you in the dirty chair and which make you stay there.

For me, a medical diagnosis of two aneurysms had me sitting in the dirty chair and allowing the trash to pile up around me. I was in danger of being so buried in negativity that I couldn't see anything outside of the reality I created for myself. Our thoughts influence our emotions, and those emotions influence how we behave. If I continued to stay in that chair, I would have remained isolated from my loved ones, I wouldn't have sought treatment, and, as my therapist said, I would have died.

I didn't, because I'm writing this book for you. So now, Let me walk you through the next steps once you know what thoughts and experiences make up your dirty chair. There's a bit of tough love coming your way, but stick with it. You have the support you need to get through this step.

After you figure out what your dirty chair is, it's time to evaluate what the thoughts and emotions are doing to your body, your relationships, and your business.

What feelings do you have as a result of the thoughts that put you in the dirty chair? How do those feelings affect your body? Do you feel like crying? Are you tense? Shaking? What physiological symptoms do you experience?

What are those feelings stopping you from doing? Are you avoiding a conversation with your spouse? Are you not growing your business because you're afraid to delegate? What are you afraid of? Leaving a job? Going against societal or parental expectations? Are you a mouse in church hiding and waiting for someone to bring you cheese? Or are you going to get that cheese?

Are you fully engaged in your potential? Are you living your purpose? Are you walking the walk? Do you like what you see? Are you planning to take all your potential to the grave? Are you willing to die with your music still inside you? Are you willing to do the work so you can engage in your truth and share your gifts with the world? Or are you going to let society and external forces keep you stuck? Are you going to let them take away your power?

How do you feel about the life you've created with those thoughts and feelings? What results are you getting? Are those the results you want? What results would you rather have? What are the opportunities for personal growth that could help you get a better result?

If you don't like what you see, it's time to make a change, bounce back from the dirty chair that keeps you stuck.

DECIDE TO GET UP

Would you believe me if I told you that the evaluation you just did was the hard part? Hopefully, you feel relieved. Once you know what your dirty chair is, how you got there, and how it's impacting your life, it's time to make a decision. Decide you are a leader who builds a successful business, decide you have a supportive and loving spouse, decide that you get to solve this medical issue and live.

I had to decide that the result of a double brain aneurysm didn't have to be death. The result could be different. If I decided to do everything in my power, I could survive. If I do my part, I could do more than survive.

Once I decided to stop letting defeat swirl around my brain and take up valuable energy, I needed to take inspired action. Inspired action is one small act that changes your momentum. For me, it was contacting a therapist and setting an appointment. That small step changed my momentum. What is your one small step?

ELICIT A SUPPORT SYSTEM

When you're trying to pull yourself out of a dirty chair, especially a dirty chair you've been in for a while, you'll need some help as you stand and more help as you move forward. Depending on what your dirty chair is, you'll need different types of support.

In my journey, I needed the support of family in caring for my son while I traveled to find the best doctors. I needed people to come to appointments with me, so I didn't miss any important information. I also needed to ensure I stayed connected to God.

Prayer is always an important part of getting me out of the dirty chair. You might call it meditation, and that's fine, as long as you remain connected and find strength in your practice. God is always working in our favor, but we have to do our part and be open to the magic. Making a decision to work for a different outcome and stop letting death consume me led me to get support. The inspired action of starting therapy helped me reach out to my friends and family, my coworkers, and create a support system that reinforced the positive momentum.

Who can be your support system? Make a list of family members, friends, and business contacts who can help you. If you lack support, make a plan for finding it. Hire a therapist, find a mentor, join a support group, or hire a coach.

FIND ALIGNMENT

Are you sick of me discussing alignment yet? I hope not, because so much of your success in life and business relies on it. The dirty chair tries to distract you from your purpose, your desires, and your vision. When you're climbing out of the dirty chair, you need to ensure your decisions align your purpose with your vision and mission. It's easy for our minds to convince us that not moving forward is the best decision.

Before I started SMPsychotherapy, I was very comfortable in life. I was a mother, and I lived in the place I wanted, I enjoyed traveling. I could have stayed there, but that decision wouldn't have aligned with my purpose, vision, or mission. I went to a job every day that didn't fulfill me. Living out of alignment makes it difficult to maintain enthusiasm and momentum in life, and you need momentum to keep you out of the dirty chair.

Finding alignment for me always involves meditation, prayer, journaling, and reading books that align with my values and point me in the direction I want to go. I also reach out to mentors, hire coaches, and surround myself with others focused on growth. Your process may be different, but it's vital that you have a process for reconnection.

The point of staying connected to your purpose is that doing so allows you to filter through the possible solutions to your problems to pick one that aligns with your purpose. My purpose is to help others heal, transform, and build a legacy they're proud of. Giving in to a brain aneurysm without a fight would not have helped me fulfill that purpose. What is your purpose? Are your decisions helping you achieve it? If not, make a different decision.

INVITE A NEW PERSPECTIVE

When you're stuck in a dirty chair and trash piles up around you in the form of negative thoughts, it can be impossible to see other perspectives. Your thoughts repeat, your emotions grow bigger and harder to ignore, and your dreams feel far out of reach. I know, I've been there.

Seeing a new perspective starts with challenging the repeating thoughts. This is where we stop focusing on the problem and start getting curious about solutions. Yes, this involves talking to yourself. You don't have to do it out loud (but I won't judge you if you do). The conversation goes something like this.

This is hopeless. I'm going to die.

"But what if you don't?"

I don't know what to do. There's just no way I can survive this.

"Is that true? Maybe you don't know what to do, but I bet you can find someone that does."

Eventually, the negative thoughts give up and disappear into the background. They're only powerful if we feed them with feeling sad, hopeless, and upset.

CREATE GOALS AND TAKE MASSIVE ACTION

Once you've gotten out of the chair, decided to move away from it, and invited in a new perspective that keeps you building momentum, it's time to make an action plan. An action plan always starts with goals. For me, the goal was to live.

Once you have a goal, you figure out what you need to do in order to accomplish it. I needed to learn as much as I could about the type of aneurysm I was dealing with. I read, I listened, I learned. I needed to meet with specialists. I needed to find a surgeon willing to operate. It took me four states and countless doctor visits before I settled on surgery near my home in Hartford, CT. My massive action plan led me to a qualified surgeon and a successful surgery that had me back on my feet and walking out of the hospital three days later.

In business, you will have adversity. You will have problems. Your new product launch will flop, your new office space will have a leak that damages your equipment, or maybe a pandemic will threaten the very fabric of your business. To jump the hurdles, to pivot, and stay on a path toward your purpose, you must develop the ability to manage your thoughts and emotions.

We have 70–80,000 thoughts a day, and most of them are repeated thoughts that influence behavior. Thoughts create images and stories in our brains. If the images and thoughts are negative, we will live in a negative space. Your behavior is what leads you to the result, the life you're living right now. If you don't like the results you're getting, you have to shift those thoughts. Once you become a gentle observer of your feelings, and connect the thoughts that stimulate those feelings, you can start to climb out of your dirty chair and make a plan for moving away from it.

It's unlikely you'll completely eliminate your dirty chair. They're constructed over years from experiences and feelings that happened long before you started a business. But you don't need to be rid of the dirty chair in order to succeed; you just need the skills for getting out of it, dusting yourself off, and taking steps forward. When you repeat this process as a leader, you become an inspiration to others, and adept at passing those skills on to the next generation.

CHAPTER TAKEAWAYS

- Everyone has a dirty chair and many of us have more than one.
- Your dirty chair is a place where negative thoughts reinforce negative emotions and leave you feeling stuck.
- When you're sitting in the dirty chair, you are out of alignment with your purpose.
- Getting out of the dirty chair requires a decision, an openness to new perspectives, support, and massive, inspired action.
- You need a self-care plan for daily use to prevent you from sitting in the dirty chair, but you also need a specialized self-care plan to pull yourself out of it.

Chapter 4

Million-Dollar Faith and Confidence

While learning how to get out of a dirty chair is important, the real progress is when you find a way to stay out of it altogether. Faith and confidence are the best ways I've found to stay out of the dirty chair. Let me explain how faith and confidence work to keep you moving forward.

At seventeen, I walked into Post University with optimism, dreams, and a full scholarship. Imagine my surprise when, a few months later, I found myself in the academic advisor's office getting a talking to about how I was going to lose my scholarship and find myself kicked out of school if I didn't get it together. What happened? How did I, a kid with a full-ride scholarship, wind up sitting in a vinyl chair across from a metal desk with a 1.8 GPA?

I thought I was doing all I could to produce excellent work. I spent days on assignments that took my native English-speaking peers an hour. I redid assignments and still couldn't seem to get them right. All through high school, trying my best had been enough, and suddenly, my drive to be excellent wasn't cutting it.

I walked out of that first meeting feeling like a deflated bounce house—unable to fulfill its purpose. I was already giving this college thing my all. I thought I couldn't meet the requirements. I thought I wasn't capable of the level of excellence needed to complete university. But I'd always seen myself as college material, as someone destined for success. I was supposed to be the first woman in my family that achieved higher education.

If my one hundred percent wasn't good enough, should I just let go of my dreams?

If you've already read Chapter 3, hopefully you recognize the dirty chair I was falling into. Embarrassment, shame, and self-doubt threatened to take me under. Thankfully, there were people around me who believed in me more than I did at that moment. I had an academic advisor and a few dedicated professors willing to guide me in a new direction and help me find a new perspective.

What was it I needed to do to start liking my result?

In high school, I took classes in a bilingual setting. This meant my instruction was provided mostly in Spanish. I was a good student, did my work, and achieved excellent grades. But I didn't become proficient at English because my classes were taught in Spanish, I spoke Spanish at home, and I was friends with other Spanish-speaking people. I spoke and understood English, but not to the degree necessary to succeed in university. What's more, I developed the tendency to isolate and do it all myself; I didn't know how to rely on resources and support. I believed I could be successful; I had the faith thing figured out. But failing shook my confidence.

Trying to do everything by myself wasn't working anymore. I became a student of "how to do university in English" and fought my way out of the 1.8 hole I'd dug for myself. Through that process, I learned that the key to accomplishing anything is what I call the faith and confidence formula.

People use the words faith and confidence in many ways, so before we continue, it's probably best if we settle on a definition for each. I define faith as an unwavering belief that something is true. Confidence is knowing without a doubt that something will happen. Faith comes first, and does not require evidence; it needs heart, prayer, and surrender. Confidence relies on evidence of success and is built over time. Confidence is when you know you've already overcome and you develop the skills to succeed. There are three types of faith and confidence you'll need to get through any situation in life and in business.

MULTI-MILLION DOLLAR FAITH AND CONFIDENCE FORMULA

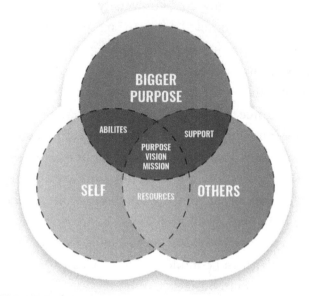

FAITH AND CONFIDENCE

Faith:
Unwavering belief that something is true. Faith comes first, and does not require evidence - it needs heart, prayer, and surrender.

Confidence:
Knowing without a doubt that something will happen. Confidence relies on evidence of success and is built over time. When you know you've already overcome and you develop the skills to succeed.

THREE TYPES OF FAITH AND CONFIDENCE:

⭐ Bigger Purpose: There is something bigger than us that gives us purpose.
Faith sounds like, "I believe God will guide me." Confidence says, "God has my back, I know he does beca

⭐ Yourself: You can do what you set your mind to.
Faith sounds like, "I believe I can do anything I want and have anything I desire." Confidence says, "I believed I could ____, and I did it, so I can do this next hard thing."

⭐ Others: Others will show up to help and guide you when you need it.
Faith sounds like, "I believe God will lead the people I need into my life." Confidence sounds like, "I've trusted this person with ___ in the past and they've never let me down."

1. There is something bigger than us that gives us purpose. Faith sounds like, "I believe God will guide me." Confidence says, "God has my back. I know he does because in the past he ..."

   I have faith that God will guide me toward the next right action in my life and business. I have confidence that if I get quiet, focus my energy, and listen, I will hear His guidance because it's happened time and time again.

2. You can do what you set your mind to. Faith sounds like, "I believe I can do anything I want and have anything I desire." Confidence says, "I believed I could _____, and I did it, so I can do this next hard thing."

   Before I decided to start writing my first book, I had faith that writing books to change people's lives was part of my purpose. Once I wrote my first one, I developed the confidence that, with the right support, I could write as many books as I wanted.

3. Others will show up to help and guide you when you need it. Faith sounds like, "I believe God will lead the people I need into my life." Confidence sounds like, "I've trusted this person with ___ in the past and they've never let me down."

   I have faith that when I need support, I will find the right people because my Creator doesn't make me work alone. I have confidence that the people I engage to support me are as committed to their work as I am to mine, and the track record of support I've gotten in the past reinforces that confidence.

I could have let failing that first semester keep me from moving forward. The temptation to give in and give up was strong. But I had purpose, I had vision, and I had opened to a new perspective. With the help of my academic advisor and Dr. Kaplan, a biology professor I still count as one of my biggest supporters, I opened up to the idea of seeking additional support. My goal was to increase my GPA, stay in school, and graduate. These were nonnegotiable.

I was no stranger to effort. I already said I burned days on assignments that should have taken hours. I didn't need to work harder; I needed to be smarter and more intentional about my work, and get the support I needed to fill in my gaps in knowledge and ability. I made a step-by-step plan for success that included all the support available at the university.

Dr. Kaplan and other professors were willing to stay after class or show up early to work with me on concepts I didn't understand. I leaned into their support. I learned about the writing center on campus and spent hours there working on every single written assignment to ensure it met the requirements. I visited the tutoring center any time I needed help. I started forming friendships with people outside the Hispanic community.

I finished the semester with a 3.5 GPA. That huge jump was because of the faith and confidence I developed in God, myself, and others. My faith made me feel comfortable and safe enough to take risks. I pushed myself, stretched my abilities, and it paid off.

It was game on. There was no way I was not going to accomplish my goals. In my four and a half years at Post University, I completed two separate degrees. I took more than 21 credits each semester to make it happen. Whenever things got tough, as they always do, I relied on my faith and confidence formula. It hasn't failed me yet.

With my coaching clients, I often notice they have trouble making the leap from one type of work to another, even when they know it's the right move. Sometimes they waver back and forth while considering adding another program to their offerings, other times it's a hesitation when they consider expanding or hiring additional staff. Sometimes, it's committing to take their business goals and dreams to the next level. Even when the data shows that their next move needs to happen, even when they want it so badly they can taste it, they hesitate, they listen to naysayers, they freeze.

Whatever your next step, you need faith and confidence to get you there. Faith will help you defrost and put one foot in front of the other until you build confidence. The more decisions you make in business, the more success you'll have and the more confident you'll become. Faith first, confidence follows.

In 2018, I was working as a school social worker when I got my license and began seeing private practice clients. I planned to see clients on evenings and weekends outside the school schedule.

I wrote my business plan using the pillars of business success I detail in Part 3 of this book and started marketing before I opened the doors. I had a waitlist of over fifty people. With that data in front of me, I had to change what I was doing.

When I decided that moving into full-time private practice was my next move, I took steps to reinforce my faith. I set affirmations and alarms on my phone to encourage me. One day in early fall, I was sitting in my office at the school and in walked Brooke, the principal.

My phone chimed, an affirmation flashing on the screen. Congratulations for quitting your job, your last day is tomorrow!

"That's impossible." Brooke rolled her eyes.

"Watch me, you never know," I answered back.

Brooke wasn't the only one who had something negative to say about my leap to private practice. Well-meaning friends and family questioned why I would leave a steady paycheck and benefits with a young child to care for. They cautioned me to go slow and do both full-time work and private practice for a while.

The data showed me I needed to do private practice full time. My intuition told me it was the right move. My desire guided me in that direction. My faith was stronger than the negativity from those around me.

I had one friend who was a business owner. When I told her about my dreams for a private practice and quitting my job, she said, "What's the worst thing that can happen? You fail? Eh, you get up and try again. What is the best thing that can happen? You make it. Take the leap, believe in God, he has your back. When you had brain surgery, he had your back, when you lost your baby, when you became a single mother. This isn't different."

This is why you need a solid support system. You need people to remind you of your past successes to renew your confidence.

A few weeks later, I handed in my resignation.

"You couldn't wait to leave, huh?" Brooke was upset.

Before I made it back to my office, the Human Resources department for the city was on the phone.

"Is there a problem going on? How much money do you want to stay? We really need bilingual social workers in our schools. Would switching to a different school help?"

My reply was simple, and based on my faith in my abilities, my higher power, and the team I had in place to support me. "There is no problem. This isn't about money, this is about purpose, and I can't fulfill my purpose here."

Faith and confidence will help you dream bigger. You can't build something from your comfort zone. You need to stretch and grow and reach higher, which is why you need that faith in something bigger than you. HE gave you this purpose, and HE will help you live it, if you do your part.

Having visions this big and leaving what feels comfortable will likely scare you-know-what out of you. Fear is a dirty chair. Don't sit in that chair too long. Don't let fear stop you from creating the life and business you desire. Become a gentle observer of your thoughts and feelings about growth, success, or your next step. How are those thoughts and emotions impacting your behaviors?

I remembered what results I was getting from working in the school system. I felt stifled. I wasn't having the impact I wanted to have. I didn't have the financial or time freedom I craved. I was not happy. I needed to face the fear and transform it into empowerment, compassion for myself, and inspiration to do more.

Faith allows you to make that transition. Faith is the key to getting out of that dirty chair. Everything is possible for you no matter what because the only thing that can hold you back from accomplishing your dreams, vision, and purpose is you.

Before you move on to the next chapter, I want to invite you to share with me your current state of faith and confidence. What area do you have the most faith and the most confidence: higher power, in yourself, and in others? What area do you struggle with faith and confidence in? Why do you think that is? Please email me at soribel@soribelmartinez.com. I will personally respond to each email.

EMAIL SORIBEL

CHAPTER TAKEAWAYS

- There are three types of faith and confidence you need to succeed in business: in a higher power, in yourself, and in others.
- Faith is trusting that God has your back, that you can do what you set your mind to, and that others will show up to support you. Faith must come first.
- Confidence develops after repeated successful experiences when you exercise your faith. You trust in God because he's shown up before, you trust in yourself because you've done this before, and you trust others because they've consistently delivered on their promises.
- Faith and confidence will help you navigate the fear that will inevitably show up as you build your business.

Chapter 5

Multi-Million-Dollar Self-Care

I 've told plenty of my own stories in the preceding chapters. I have plenty of stories about how self-care impacts my life and business, but for this chapter, I want to introduce you to one of my business coaching clients. When I first met Erin, she struggled with exhaustion, stress, and burnout. Her many responsibilities included maintaining her own business, working a regular job, homeschooling her kids, and caring for her aging parents. All this leads to anxiety and migraines. Despite struggling with her responsibilities, Erin still wanted to do good in the world but didn't know where to start.

Erin's struggles had taken a toll on her business, and she wasn't making the money she wanted to make. She could trace this back to several errors. She didn't have the proper business systems in place. She had no marketing plan. She had no business model in place. She was trying to do most of the work herself. Finally, the people doing her bookkeeping had made a mess of them, causing additional headaches and hours of work to fix.

Making matters worse, as she scrambled to keep up, she missed more time with her family, causing problems in her relationships. Every area of her life was a mess.

This is a long list of problems, but all trace back to one foundational issue: self-care. As a business owner, you are the business. You are the brand. When you are drained, your business is lacking. When you are disorganized, your business is in disarray. The success of your business is dependent on how well you function.

Running on empty, Erin was far from thriving in her business. As a result, her mental and emotional state affected her whole life. She didn't have the mental capacity or energy to manage day-to-day operations or think strategically. She couldn't thrive until she got the mental space she needed and the proper support around her.

Your business thrives when you serve from a place of abundance, success, and excellence. Erin had not yet learned this. Instead, Erin learned the lesson so many of us learn from our parents, religion and society—to be a good person you must constantly serve others with little regard for yourself. How many people do you know who run a business and can't seem to find time to go to the gym, cook a healthy meal, or spend an afternoon with their family? Plenty. I know I already said it, but it bears repeating. You are your business. If you are exhausted, your business will be sluggish. Fixing your business requires you to first fix your self-care.

Erin's story is not unique. Too many business owners push themselves to exhaustion without realizing the damage they are doing to themselves, their relationships, and the business. Taking care of yourself first is crucial for those wanting to thrive in business and serve clients well.

To build a Multi-Million-Dollar Self-Care Plan, you must take deliberate actions to improve your spiritual, physical, mental, and emotional health and relationships. Unfortunately, many people view self-care as superficial or a selfish act that takes away from their responsibilities to others. This is an error in judgment. Self-care is not selfish, and is, in fact, a necessary practice for overall health and success. It is a top priority, and here are some reasons why that's true:

- You cannot pour from an empty cup: When you neglect your self-care needs, you become depleted and drained. Taking time for self-care replenishes your energy, allowing you to be more present and effective in your personal and professional lives.

- You are the foundation of your business: As a business owner, you are the face of your brand. By prioritizing self-care, you are strengthening the foundation of your business and setting yourself up for long-term success.

- You are setting an example for others: When you prioritize self-care, you are modeling healthy behavior for others in your life, including your children, employees, and loved ones.

- You are taking responsibility for your health: Neglecting self-care can lead to burnout, physical illness, mental health issues, and many other problems. Taking responsibility for your health through self-care practices prevents these negative outcomes and creates a healthier, more sustainable life for yourself and others.

When developing a self-care plan, it is crucial to understand that the task is neither short nor simple. A self-care plan needs to

be thorough, in-depth, and, most of all, effective. It includes care for all the areas previously mentioned:
- Spiritual
- Mental
- Emotional
- Physical
- Relationships

It is not adequate to focus on one or two of these areas. A multi-million-dollar self-care plan includes all five areas. Therefore, I want to explore each one.

SPIRITUAL

We are spiritual beings. We need to connect with something bigger than ourselves to fulfill our purpose. Think about how a flower must be connected to the source to thrive. If you pluck the flower from the soil, it soon dies. Business owners must prioritize their spiritual connection to stay connected to their source and purpose and prevent their lives from withering.

Spiritual self-care is about nurturing your spirit and soul by taking actions that honor your values, beliefs, and purpose. You can achieve it through various practices such as meditation, yoga, prayer, or spending time in nature. By taking the time to quiet your mind and reconnect with your inner self, you can tap into your spiritual essence and find inner peace and clarity.

Aspects of a healthy spiritual self-care practice include the following:

1. *Gratitude:* Being grateful is a mindset and an attitude that fosters positive energy and attracts abundance in your life. By cultivating a practice of gratitude, you can shift your

focus from what is lacking to what you already have, and this can help you feel more content and fulfilled.

2. *Forgiveness:* When we hold on to grudges and negative emotions towards others, it can block your spiritual growth and hinder your ability to connect with our higher self. By practicing forgiveness, you release these negative emotions and create space for love, compassion, and understanding. You can release that person to be themselves while you move on to your destiny. This can be a powerful way to heal and find strength.

3. *Alignment:* Everything in your life needs to be aligned with your values and purpose. Living your life with purpose creates a sense of meaning and fulfillment that nurtures your spirit. By making choices that align with your values, you honor your authentic self and live a life that is true to who you are.

MENTAL

Another crucial aspect of self-care is our mental health and psychological functioning. If we are dealing with depression, anxiety, or any type of disorder, it will hinder every area of our life, including your business.

There are several practices that can assist you in your journey of mental health. Here are some of them:

1. *Mindfulness.* Mindfulness is the practice of being fully present and engaged in the present moment without judgment. It involves paying attention to our thoughts and feelings without getting caught up in them. Practicing mindfulness can cultivate a greater sense of self-awareness and emotional regulation.

2. *Boundaries:* Boundaries are limits you set for yourself and others in your personal and professional life. They are essential for maintaining healthy relationships and reducing stress. When you set healthy boundaries, you can prioritize your mental health and well-being by avoiding situations and people that drain you.

3. *Therapy and counseling:* Seeking professional help for mental health concerns is crucial to maintaining good mental health. Therapy and counseling provide a safe space to talk about your thoughts and feelings with a trained professional who can provide you with tools and strategies to manage any mental health issues.

4. *Time off:* Self-care involves taking breaks and engaging in activities that promote relaxation and reduce stress. This could be anything from walking in nature, meditating, or engaging in a hobby you enjoy. By taking time to relax and recharge, you can prevent burnout and maintain good mental health.

EMOTIONAL

Imposter syndrome, limiting beliefs, low self-esteem, and fear can all hinder your business and your personal life. Emotional self-care involves recognizing, processing, and expressing your emotions in healthy and constructive ways.

One of the most crucial aspects of emotional self-care is practicing self-awareness. This means paying attention to how you feel, why you feel that way, and how your emotions affect your thoughts and behaviors. Self-awareness helps to identify negative emotions and take steps to manage them before they escalate.

There are practices you can develop to improve your emotional health. Here are some of them:

1. *Self-compassion:* This involves treating yourself with kindness, understanding, and patience when you are experiencing difficult emotions. It means giving yourself permission to feel your feelings and acknowledging that it's okay to not always be okay. Self-compassion allows you to care for yourself during challenging times and helps avoid self-criticism and self-judgment.

2. *Coping mechanisms:* This involves behaviors or strategies you can use to deal with stress and difficult emotions. Examples of healthy coping mechanisms include journaling, exercise, spending time with loved ones, and engaging in hobbies or creative activities. These strategies help you process your emotions and find healthy ways to manage them.

3. *Learning to say no:* This means being honest with yourself and others about your emotional capacity and understanding your limits. Only say yes to those things in alignment with your values and purpose. This practice helps avoid emotional burnout and creates mental space to thrive.

PHYSICAL

Physical self-care involves:
- Seeing a doctor and dentist regularly
- Addressing health issues as they arise
- Eating well
- Getting enough sleep
- Exercising

Fresh air and sunshine can also improve your overall well-being and energy levels. Let's explore some essential activities for physical self-care.

1. *Sleep:* Lack of sleep can affect your mood, cognitive abilities, and immune system. To promote good sleep, establish a regular sleep schedule, create a sleep-conducive environment, and avoid screens and stimulating activities before bedtime.

2. *Exercise:* Regular exercise can help improve cardiovascular health, increase muscle mass, and improve mood. Check with your doctor about the proper exercise regime for you, and then set it in your schedule like any other appointment.

3. *Nutrition:* A balanced diet that includes a variety of fruits, vegetables, lean proteins, and whole grains can provide the necessary nutrients for the body to function optimally. Staying hydrated by drinking enough water is also important for physical health.

4. *Medical care:* self-care practices can include regular check-ups with healthcare providers, taking medications as prescribed, and managing any chronic health conditions. Regular healthcare practices can also prevent illnesses and diseases, so you can keep working.

RELATIONSHIPS

It is essential to nurture your connections with partners, friends, and family. Parents must prioritize their relationships with their children, giving time for bonding, instruction, support, and play. Physical intimacy with your partner is also vital and requires time and emotional connection.

To help you in the area of intimacy, use the QR code here to download my intimacy discovery kit.

INTIMACY RECOVERY KIT

Ignoring relationships for the sake of your business will ultimately cause suffering in your personal life and in your business. When your relationships fall apart, it affects your emotional, mental, and even physical well-being. This depleted state will ultimately weaken your business. Healthy, happy relationships fill your cup and allow you to serve out of abundance.

THE PLAN FOR ERIN

As I worked with Erin to explore all these areas, we developed a comprehensive plan to address all five of these areas. Her plan included the following:

- Therapy
- Craniosacral therapy
- Journaling
- Tapping
- Books on self-development
- Conferences to get her out of the house and network
- Meditation
- Taking time for herself
- Hiking
- Bike rides
- Lunch dates with her husband
- Stopping work at a specific time each day

- Organization systems
- Scheduling
- Setting boundaries with clients
- Delegation

Look carefully at this list. As you develop your self-care plan, yours may look different. Still, this list contains many activities and practices that are common for any effective self-care strategy. Issues such as organization systems, proper boundaries, and delegation are essential for every business owner.

In order to set those boundaries and get the support you need, ask yourself two essential questions:

Who are the toxic people in your life? Remove them.

One of the essential aspects of self-care is assessing the people in your life and identifying the toxic ones. Toxic individuals can be draining and emotionally exhausting, hindering your personal and professional growth. Recognize these people, set boundaries, and, when necessary, remove them from your life.

Who are the support people in your life? If you don't have them, buy them. (Yep, you can buy the support you need!)

A support system is a must. Everyone needs help to navigate life's challenges. A support network can provide support in every area of life and business. If you don't have the support you need, hire professionals. Coaches, therapists, and administrative support staff are all essential. Don't make excuses. Get the help you need to thrive.

After working with Erin, her life and business changed. Her business was under control, her health improved in every area, and her relationships grew stronger. Yet I don't want you to just take my word for it. Erin has agreed to be interviewed, so you can hear it all from her. Here is what Erin had to say:

Me: Tell me about how you felt in life and business before working with me.

Erin: Scattered. I didn't have an accountability buddy and was trying to do it all. I didn't understand which issues were mine and which issues were the responsibility of other people. I didn't have an understanding of when I needed to get involved and when I could step back. I was a fixer. I scuttled around like a squirrel, which wasn't serving me. I was drained and overwhelmed, having migraines and experiencing digestive symptoms. I never said no because I didn't know how to say no.

Me: And what did you hope to gain when you came to me for coaching?

Erin: I wanted clarity. I wanted the ability to be direct but kind when it came to conflict. I wanted a healthy relationship with conflict instead of avoidance. I also wanted a better understanding of business issues like branding. How do I represent myself and my business?

Me: So to accomplish those things and more, we developed your unbreakable self-care plan. Say a little about that plan.

Erin: Sure. I started journaling more, stepping away from arguments, and tracking my body. I learned that if my face gets hot, I step away instead of arguing. I practiced EFT (Emotional Freedom

Technique) and tapping. I also learned to slow down and how to advocate for my needs. For example, I communicate if I need help, solutions, or just a listening ear. Sometimes, all I need is to breathe and get a hug.

I also worked on setting boundaries. I learned that when I feel overwhelmed or get a headache, it tells me I need a boundary. This one created some issues. Since I haven't been good at boundaries, people don't know I'm trying to set them. They expect me to always be available. That means I have to practice holding boundaries, like when my mom texts me four times a day, and I'm working and can't talk to her.

Me: But you've learned to hold those boundaries. It's been great to see your strength in that area. Now that you have been practicing self-care, how does your plan support your life, work, and purpose?

Erin: Now I am clear on what I'm good at on the business team. I am better at letting other people do their own work. I'm learning new skills like relationship-building, promotions, and pricing. I finally know my worth.

I also let my family members do tasks that suit them. I focus on my area of genius, like being a goddess of relationships and community, and finding ways other people can contribute. I get energy from interactions with others and from promotions. I thrive when I see the big picture, dream, and vision. I love visualizing what the business will be in five years. Since I'm a visionary, I spend more time improving those skills. I make solid decisions and take action on my big plans. With better boundaries, I also feel more confident advocating for my own needs.

Me: You are sounding much more confident now that you have an unbreakable self-care plan.

Erin: I am. I've learned how to advocate for my own needs. I state what I can do, set a boundary, and I'm not doing anymore. As a visionary leader and business owner, I must respect my thinking time. Managing, thinking, and being in relationships take work and mental load. I need to be thoughtful in setting aside time for planning, thinking, and journaling. I have to give myself space. I've learned that a business coach, therapist, and thought partner are vital because we cannot do all the work ourselves. You can't know everything. Find your team. The person who does it all gets a migraine and throws up.

As I reflect on Erin's story and the many other journeys I have witnessed as a coach, I am reminded of the power of transformation. It is remarkable to see a person blossom from a state of uncertainty to one of self-assurance, from a place of exhaustion to one of vitality. Your story of life and business is unique, yet it needs to share a common thread with Erin and others—a commitment to self-care.

In a world that often glorifies the hustle and the endless pursuit of success, it is easy to forget that you are not an invincible being. You are human, with finite energy and real-life needs. I will say it again; you cannot pour from an empty cup. The wisdom of self-care is a guiding light in your pursuit of business success.

Imagine a life where you wake up each morning feeling refreshed and ready to tackle the day's challenges. Picture yourself radiating a sense of inner peace and contentment, grounded in the knowledge that you have taken care of yourself first. Envision your relationships flourishing as you bring your best self to every interaction. This is not a far-fetched dream. It is a reality within reach.

Self-care is the secret ingredient to unlocking your true potential. It is the fuel that propels you forward, igniting your creativity, sharpening your focus, and fostering resilience in the face of adversity. Your self-care plan becomes the blueprint for a life well-lived, where success is not just measured by external achievements, but by the quality of your life.

Your Multi-Million-Dollar Self-Care Plan creates a solid foundation where your business can thrive. You are balanced, seamlessly juggling your professional aspirations with your personal growth. The clarity and perspective that accompany a nurtured mind, body, and spirit empower you to make sound decisions and embrace opportunities with confidence.

The path to business success is not paved with sacrifice and exhaustion, but with self-care and holistic well-being. Embrace the knowledge that you are worthy of a life filled with abundance, success, and excellence, with self-care as your method of achieving it.

CHAPTER TAKEAWAYS

- You are your business and finding success requires that you care for yourself to avoid burnout.
- Self-care is multifaceted and includes your spiritual, mental, emotional, physical, and relationship needs.
- Neglecting any area of self-care will show up in your business as a lack of focus, lack of drive, lack of trust, or the inability to make decisions.
- You must create a self-care plan for every day, as well as another for when strong emotions or life-changing experiences throw you off.

Part 2

Business Fundamentals

The first part of this book is all mindset—how to think like a successful leader and business owner. The next part blends some additional mindset work with practical strategies every business owner needs to understand in order to position their business for success and growth. As you read, think about how you can incorporate these strategies into your business. Don't be afraid to dream big here, and jot notes about those dreams in the margins, on a notebook, or on the back of your hand. We will use those notes in part three as we get into the MMDPP Framework™ that will guide your success.

Chapter 6

Multi-Million-Dollar SGOT Analysis

A s a business owner, you need to be prepared to make difficult decisions about your business every day. You'll need to decide who to serve, who to hire, what services to offer, and how to change and grow your practice. So, how does a business owner make educated decisions with confidence? An SGOT analysis is a tool for figuring out the next right move for you and your business. Let's dive into how it works.

An SGOT analysis evaluates the strengths, growth areas, opportunities, and threats for your business. As a business owner, I also encourage you to do an SGOT analysis on yourself. I also encourage you to do an SGOT analysis at regular intervals, as well as anytime things feel stale or out of alignment.

Your business plan is a living document that describes your business today and explains where it is going. It is your dream and your action plan on paper. Your business plan will change often. Mine changes every time I do an SGOT analysis.

Let's walk through how to do an SGOT analysis and discuss how you use the results to create or revise a business plan.

An SGOT analysis is a mental journey, although at first you'll want to write down your thoughts until you get used to doing them. The reason I encourage business owners to complete an SGOT analysis on themselves as well as their businesses is because, as the CEO of a company, you are a separate entity from the business, but the business will reflect your own physical and mental health. The way you manage your own life, the way you support yourself, is the way you manage and support your business.

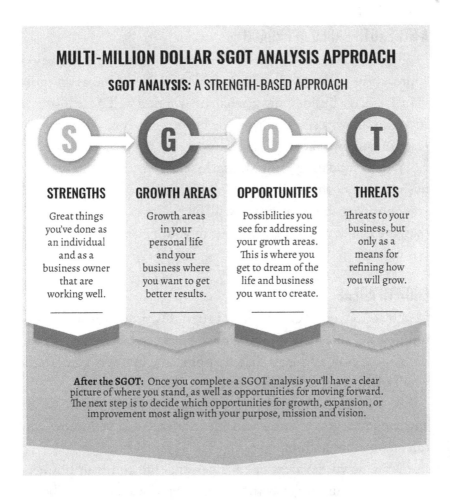

MULTI-MILLION DOLLAR SGOT ANALYSIS APPROACH

SGOT ANALYSIS: A STRENGTH-BASED APPROACH

STRENGTHS	GROWTH AREAS	OPPORTUNITIES	THREATS
Great things you've done as an individual and as a business owner that are working well.	Growth areas in your personal life and your business where you want to get better results.	Possibilities you see for addressing your growth areas. This is where you get to dream of the life and business you want to create.	Threats to your business, but only as a means for refining how you will grow.

After the SGOT: Once you complete a SGOT analysis you'll have a clear picture of where you stand, as well as opportunities for moving forward. The next step is to decide which opportunities for growth, expansion, or improvement most align with your purpose, mission and vision.

For each component of the SGOT analysis, consider your spiritual, family, and internal life. Then, for your business, consider each area of your business plan. How is your business faring in the areas of finances, marketing, alignment, and systems? Do you have all the support you need to run and scale your business the way you want?

A STRENGTH-BASED APPROACH

The SGOT analysis encourages you to use a strength-based approach to understand the great things you've done as an individual and as a business owner that are working well. Starting with strengths allows us to evaluate our business and ourselves from a place of empowerment.

When evaluating your strengths and the strengths of your business, write them all down. Seeing the areas where you and your business shine on paper will fill you with encouragement that you can conquer the next step in your personal life and your business.

GROWTH AREAS

The acronym SGOT stands for strengths, growth areas, opportunities, and threats. The term growth areas can be problematic for the same reason a strength-based approach empowers you. That's why I often use the term growth areas.

Your business mindset is your growth mindset on steroids, so any supposed growth areas you identify are areas you know you can learn, grow, and improve.

Write down the areas in your personal life and your business where you want to get better results. Maybe that means being in better physical health and finding a way to increase traffic to your website. Move through this part of the SGOT quickly. You don't want to dwell on growth areas because that will stifle your momentum. Use these growth areas to fuel change in your life and business.

OPPORTUNITIES

The opportunities you list are possibilities you see for addressing your growth areas, or growth areas. This is where you get to dream of the life and business you want to create. This is the second most important area of the SGOT (second only to the strengths portion) because dreams can fuel your desire to action.

Going back to the growth areas we identified above, can you add in another session every week at the gym to improve your physical health? How will hiring a web-developer enhance the website and increase traffic? Could you add more marketing efforts to fill your calendar and make your practice more profitable? Don't pick any single idea here. Use it as a brainstorm that you will narrow down after completing the SGOT.

THREATS

As a business owner, I'm guided by my purpose, so I don't pay too much attention to how other practitioners run their business. I do what feels right for me, my employees, and our clients based on our current strengths and business trends. However, identifying potential threats to your business is vital.

Threats to your business can come from many directions. Your physical health may be a threat to your business, especially if the systems you have in place rely on you being involved in every part of the business. Threats may also come from external forces such as what is happening in society. The COVID-19 pandemic was a direct threat to many therapy practices and ignoring it would have caused my business to go under. Write down the threats to your business, but only as a means for refining how you will grow.

AFTER THE SGOT

Completing an SGOT analysis will empower you to make better decisions, act swiftly, and create a plan for growing as an individual and as a business.

Once you complete an SGOT analysis, you'll have a clear picture of where you stand, as well as opportunities for moving forward. The next step is to decide which opportunities for growth, expansion, or improvement most align with your purpose, mission, and vision.

Some of the SGOT analyses I've completed in the course of my business led me to the following actions:

- Moving from a solo practice to a group practice
- Changing from in-person services to telehealth
- Adding business coaching services
- Adding concierge therapy services
- Adding medication management services
- Adding additional marketing efforts
- Writing a book
- Writing another book
- Changing the customer journey to be more personalized
- Refining my hiring and onboarding processes

Every single action I've taken as a result of my SGOT analysis helped me grow as a leader and helped my business search and serve more people. If you want more on the SGOT analysis, I invite you to download my SGOT guide using this link.

Often what holds people back from making these decisions is a mindset full of limiting beliefs about how they can show up in the world and what they should do and want. In the next chapter,

I'll dive into some more mindset work to help position you as a leader in your field. Fixing mindset issues before diving into the MMDPP Framework™ will ensure you're building a solid business foundation.

CHAPTER TAKEAWAYS

- An SGOT analysis is a strengths-based practice you can use to make decisions about your personal life and your business.
- Doing an SGOT analysis regularly can ensure you make decisions in alignment with your purpose, vision, and mission.
- Strengths are the basis for your next decision and your next success. Focusing on strengths first keeps you in an empowered mindset.
- Growth areas are those places where you can grow as an individual and as a business owner.
- Opportunities combine growth areas with the resources available to you now. Business owners must always look out for opportunities for expansion, growth, and development.
- Threats to your business may be internal or external, but acknowledging them allows you to plan for a quick detour from your plan to address issues before they overwhelm your business.
- An SGOT analysis will help you set the right goals for your life and business.

Chapter 7

Multi-Million-Dollar
Money Mindset

W hat is your money story? Before you respond with "I don't have one," or "what does that have to do with starting a private therapy practice?" Just as everyone has a story about mental health, career prospects, and relationships, everyone has a money story. That story either helps you create greater wealth and impact, or it holds you back from reaching your potential. To illustrate this point, let me share my old money story.

Growing up, there were two main influences on my money story. First was my father. He was a businessman and someone I looked up to in many ways. He was not, however, good at managing his personal financial resources. Papi lost everything, including his home, because he could not properly manage his money. I feared I would have the same money behaviors as my father. I was afraid of having too much money and not managing it well, and I was terrified of not having enough money to support myself and my family.

In addition to Papi, my money mindset was heavily influenced by the Pentecostal Church my mother joined when I was nine years old. In addition to regulating the length of our skirts and the people we were allowed to spend time with, the church had strong ideas about money and financial success.

Through the Pentecostal church, I learned that money is the root of all evil. If a person made too much money, it would change them (and not for the better). Money would make you greedy and sinful and bar your entry to heaven.

These two experiences—losing everything because of a lack of money management skills and learning that money would prevent me from accessing heaven—combined in my young brain to form a complicated money story that kept me from embracing a path to financial success. See, I always wanted to make a lot of money. Sure, I wanted a nice car, and amazing shoes, but that's not the only thing money can do. Money can help us create a massive positive impact on the world. I wanted to create an incredible life for my son, send him to private school, have a comfortable home to live in, and have enough money left over to do something positive in the world. I wanted all of this, and I was afraid to go for it.

My money story made me afraid of losing everything because of poor management of my money, but I also feared success. Financial success would change me as a person, invite judgment from my family and loved ones, and deliver me straight to Hell.

So, how did I get from that money story to a business owner bringing in millions of dollars in revenue each year, driving my dream car, and financing a private school education for the incredible young man I'm raising?

I decided.

That's it. Like so many pieces of this book, success begins with deciding. Remember in Chapter 3 when I introduced the concept of the dirty chair? We all have more than one. For me, my old money story was a dirty chair. Getting out of it started with a decision.

You can also decide to create a new story about how money works in your life. You can see money as a positive force instead of something to be feared. Money can be something you manage instead of something that controls your life. Money can be a source of joy rather than stress.

MILLION-DOLLAR MONEY MINDSET FRAMEWORK™

WHAT'S YOUR MONEY STORY?

IDENTIFY THE LIMITING BELIEF

* Identify the belief that's holding you back.
* Helps you shift those beliefs
* Create the relationship with money that serves you

WHAT IS YOUR MONEY STORY?

* Observe the experiences you had that created the belief about money you identified

IDENTIFYING THE PERSON/PEOPLE WHO MOST INFLUENCED YOUR MONEY BELIEFS

* Identify people who have helped create or reinforce your money mindset.
* Identify the people and institutions who influenced your mindset.
* Decide to release their influence.
* Release other people's expectations, ideas, and issues with money and create your own.

1. Identifying the limiting belief.

   The first step to changing your mindset about anything, whether it's exercise, money, or your marriage, is to identify the belief that's holding you back. You may have more than one. I believed I wouldn't be able to manage money, and that having money would make me evil. Identifying your current beliefs about money can help you shift those beliefs so you can create the relationship with money that serves you.

2. What is your money story?

Observe the experiences you had that created the belief about money you identified. For me, this meant remembering the fights I witnessed my parents have about money. I remembered the sermons about the evils of money. Do you have a money story influenced by your parents? Is your money story from the way society says women and money should interact?

3. Identifying the person/people who most influenced your money beliefs.

Just as you have a money story, you have people who have helped create or reinforce your money mindset. This may be a specific person, such as my Papi, or it might be an organization like a church. For some people, your money mindset is influenced by your career choice—mental health professionals are supposed to help people, not make lots of money, right?

4. Identify the people and institutions who influenced your mindset. Then, decide to release their influence. Just because Papi wasn't good with money doesn't mean I won't be. It's not genetic. Just because other therapists don't want to build a profitable private practice doesn't mean you can't. You don't own their beliefs. You only own yours. Release other people's expectations, ideas, and issues with money and create your own.

WHAT IS THE MEANING YOU GAVE TO THAT STORY?

Somehow, you internalized the struggles surrounding money that others had as your own. You took on an identity related to money that isn't yours. If it was yours, it would feel authentic to you and the way you want to live your life.

HOW DOES YOUR MONEY MINDSET IMPACT YOUR LIFE AND BUSINESS?

I invite you to keep this question open in your mind for at least a week. How does your money story impact your decisions about purchasing, investing, sharing, and saving money? How does your money story show up at home with your friends and family? How does your money story impact the decision you make as a business owner?

HOW CAN YOU RELEASE THE PERSON OR PEOPLE WHO INFLUENCED YOUR MONEY MINDSET?

Deciding to release the person or people who influenced your money story doesn't mean removing them from your life, though you're free to do that. What I mean by release is that you no longer identify with that story, you no longer take that person's experiences with money as your own and you don't allow them to influence how you behave with and around money. Releasing others is granting yourself freedom from anyone else's money story and granting yourself permission to create your own story about how money works for you.

CRAFT YOUR IDEAL MONEY MINDSET

Once you decide not to hold on to other people's money stories, you get to decide how you want money to work in your life. I wanted to build a profitable business that allowed me to create a comfortable lifestyle where money was never the reason I said no to something I wanted for me or my son. I wanted to make enough money to start and run a nonprofit that would positively impact the world.

My new mindset is that money is not good or bad; money is energy. Energy has no feeling attached to it. It exists for us to use, enjoy, and share. If money is energy, then it is not moral. It is just a resource that allows us to take care of ourselves, our families, and our communities. Money allows us to inject energy into the world so others can benefit. Money is meant to be spent, saved, invested, and spread around.

What is your new money mindset? How does money work in your life? (This should be a space where you allow yourself to dream a bit. Your old money story will try to stop you from dreaming—tell that old story to stop speaking. You're busy creating a new paradigm of how money works in your life.

CREATE A LEARNING PLAN AND AN ACTION PLAN

The next step, after deciding on your new money mindset, is to work diligently to rewire the neuro-pathways that feed your old money story. Those thoughts that popped up when you tried to create your new money mindset in the previous step are there because your old neuro-pathways are still present in your brain. You have the word money linked to fear, stress, scarcity, and despair. We need to work to connect the word money to joy, ease, flow, and generosity instead.

The first step to rewiring neural-pathways is education. You need to create a money mindset education program for yourself. This can include books, conferences, online courses, and connecting with others who have the money mindset you want for yourself. For a list of my favorite money mindset resources, visit my website using the QR code below.

MONEY MINDSET RESOURCES

In my education journey about money, I learned about the energy and frequency of money. I learned how religion and society shape our beliefs about money. I learned how society tries to dictate what jobs we can have, how much money we can make, and what sort of life we can build. Then I learned to ignore all of that external noise.

I learned to shift the religious belief that money changes people. The truth is that good people do good things with money, and bad people do bad things with money. It's not the money that influences behavior. Your values do; it's who you are at your core that matters. When I started making enough money to support my family, I didn't hesitate to start a nonprofit foundation and funnel some of the revenue I earned into doing work to increase my impact on the world.

JC's Precious Minds Foundation helps single mothers with special needs children in the Dominican Republic get their children the services they need, and gives them the opportunity to return to school or start their own businesses so they can thrive. My purpose is to help others live a fulfilling life, and having financial resources allows me to help others and further my purpose, vision, and mission.

Now, I surround myself with people who have a similar view of money—people who aren't afraid of it, and know there is enough of it to go around. I have reprogrammed my brain and created new neural-pathways. This doesn't mean my old ideas about money never come up—all mindset work is continuous—but now I have new neural-pathways that allow me to easily shut down limiting beliefs and refocus my attention where it matters. I no longer believe I will lose everything. I believe everything is possible. I am a good manager of everything that God the universe provides for me.

There is another shift that takes place when you shift your money mindset; it's a shift in your perception of your own value. Through this process, you will learn that you are valuable because you are. Your money, your business, and your accomplishments don't increase your value and your failures don't decrease your value. You are valuable because you were created.

The right money mindset is essential as you move through the rest of this book. Don't speed ahead. Rather, spend time creating your money mindset before you move through productivity, dominating the market, and the Multi-Million-Dollar Private Practice Framework™. The right mindset will make the rest of this work possible.

CHAPTER TAKEAWAYS

- Everyone has a money story. That story is created through experiences we have had surrounding money and the meaning we give to those experiences.
- Understanding how your money story impacts your life and business goals is the first step toward cultivating a million-dollar money mindset.

- Somewhere along your life path, a person or group of people influenced your money story. Figuring out who they were and what power they held in your life can help you recover.
- Getting real about how your money mindset impacts your life and business may require you to admit to some unsavory truths; do it even though it's hard.
- Cultivating a new, healthier mindset about money starts with making a decision.
- Money is energy. It is meant to be spent, shared, invested, saved, and used to create impact in our world.

Chapter 8

Productivity Is Not Just Busy

W hen people see all I do, some ask if I work twenty-four hours a day. I run a successful and growing business, work with clients, supervise staff, and impact the community. I am an author, keynote speaker, and business coach. I provide an educational blog and work to provide superior service to my clients. Beyond my business, I have a personal life, a family life, and a spiritual life while loving all that I do.

So for those wondering if I work an excessive number of hours, I do not. I am confident that I am not working as hard or as much as many other business owners. I am not busy. I am not rushed. I finish projects. I am always on time, and I do it without high levels of stress.

There is one word that makes all of this possible. That word is productivity.

There is a distinction between being busy and being productive. Learning the difference between the two and choosing productivity makes all the difference in your life and business.

In this chapter, I will show you how to get more done in less time, with less stress, and be empowered in the process. If you are currently overwhelmed with overdue tasks and constant crises, it may sound impossible, but it is not. You don't have to spend your days putting out fires and struggling to catch up. Things can change, and I will show you how.

A DAY IN MY LIFE

My Monday schedule is set with intention and forethought. I want to be empowered every Monday to set the tone for the week ahead. I will tell you exactly what I do, but first, it is essential to understand that this empowering Monday schedule starts well before that day.

To be productive on any given day requires that the day fit into a larger plan and align with your purpose. I begin by knowing what I want to accomplish over the course of the year. As I break down these goals, it leads to activities that need to be the focus quarterly, monthly, weekly, and daily energy.

I never approach a day reacting to what it will bring. Of course, if there are true emergencies, I address them, but when planning is done right, emergencies will be few and infrequent. By planning a yearly, quarterly, monthly, weekly, and daily schedule, each day fits into the plan, which always fits into my purpose, vision, mission, and passion.

Then, I always look at my schedule the night before. I use this time to adjust my mindset for what I need to accomplish the next day. Having the proper mindset empowers me to approach the day with a calm attitude and the assurance that I know exactly how to be productive that day.

By doing my mindset work, I set how I want to feel about my day and week ahead. I want to feel empowered and energetic, so that is how I develop my mindset. I plan Monday with a bang because that sets the feel for the rest of the week.

When Monday arrives, I strategically begin my day with what I love to do the most: writing. Writing my books gives me energy. Teaching is the closest I can be to my creator. It is my passion and my purpose. Beginning Monday with my writing leads to feeling empowered in a way that carries me through my week.

As I put the book aside and begin to see Monday clients, my schedule is intentional. My appointments on Monday are with some of the clients I enjoy the most. As I see their progress, I am continually reminded of my purpose and mission.

By the time my Monday draws to a close, I am infused with my purpose and passion because I have strategically planned my day to empower me. This makes all the difference in the week ahead. I start my week on a high, living out what I love to do most. Yet my Monday strategy is just one of the elements I use for productivity.

FROM THE BEGINNING

When I started my private practice, I knew I needed to specialize and be specific about my services. It is impossible to be good at everything, and I knew there was no way to be productive if I worked all over the place. I wanted to work in my area of genius and passion.

This means I needed to specialize. There are significant advantages to specializing, including the following:

- **Increased Efficiency:** When a business specializes, it can optimize its operations and processes to deliver its product or service more efficiently. Your business can focus its resources on a specific area of expertise and become more proficient in delivering high-quality outcomes. This can lead to reduced costs, higher productivity, and better customer satisfaction.

- **Competitive Advantage:** Specializing in a particular area can help your business differentiate itself from competitors. By becoming the go-to provider for a specific service, you can develop a reputation for expertise and reliability. This can attract more customers and help you to stand out in a crowded marketplace.

- **Higher Margins:** Specializing in a particular service can allow a business to charge higher prices. Customers are often willing to pay more for a specialized product or service that meets their specific needs.

- **Innovation:** Focusing on a particular area can enable your business to become a leader in that field. This can lead to more opportunities for innovation and the development of new services. This can lead to a sustainable competitive advantage and long-term growth.

Knowing these advantages, my first step was to do market research in comparison to my own strengths. I know my strengths and growth areas because of my thorough SGOT analysis. Based on this information, I decided to focus my practice and marketing on women and families. The reasoning behind this decision included the following:

- Women are usually the head of the household in terms of seeking services for the rest of the family. It's not that I won't work with men, but I know that women are often the initiator when it comes to looking for services on behalf of the men in their lives. By focusing my practice and marketing on women and families, I am working smarter, not harder.

- I understand my ideal client. I can easily attract women to my practice, and I enjoy the empowerment theory that makes the choice to change more manageable.

- Empowerment theory is based on the assumption that people have the potential to change their lives and the world around them. The approach emphasizes the importance of creating supportive environments that foster people's ability to take action and make changes. Empowerment theory teaches that individuals are more likely to become empowered when they have access to resources such as education, healthcare, social networks, and economic opportunities. Empowerment also comes from having a sense of control over one's life, having a voice in decision-making, and being part of a supportive community.

- This is where my strengths lie. I know how to create those supportive environments, and I excel at education and accessing resources. This theoretical approach helps me empower other women and helps them transform their lives.

- By knowing my ideal client is women and families, I know what language they speak. I know their needs and desires. I am not guessing or grasping at every shiny object. I know exactly how to market my private practice to women and families and connect with them authentically with minimal effort.

Knowing all this, I planned my year. I know who I serve, why I serve them, what I offer them, and what experience I want them to have. This makes planning easy. I can set my yearly goals with the needs of my clients in mind and know the abilities I have to serve them. I see the big picture and set that as my yearly goal. I then break it down into quarterly, monthly, weekly, and daily goals. This helps me to avoid being frantic or spending my days putting out fires. I am clear on my purpose, vision, and mission, and this dictates what I do every day.

Therefore, if you are ready to leave behind the frantic world of busyness and embrace the productive life, start by understanding the following:

- Who you are, including your strengths, growth areas, passions, and purpose
- The ideal client you want to serve
- What you can do to serve your clients
- The experience you want to provide

By doing these things, you will be on the path to productivity, which is entirely different from just being busy.

PRODUCTIVE VERSUS BUSY

Business owners often find themselves reacting to events, feeling frantic, rushed, and distracted. This can lead to making decisions out of stress and resorting to multitasking, which may seem like a time saver but is actually the opposite.

Multitasking is impossible. No one can entirely focus on several things simultaneously. Multitasking leads to being busy with no productivity, which becomes demoralizing. At the end of the day, you see that little or nothing has been accomplished. This can take a toll on a person's self-esteem.

Are you feeling tired, burned out, struggling to think clearly, and feeling bad about yourself and your business? In that case, it's likely you are busy and not productive. Some mistakenly assume that this is simply the life of a hardworking businessperson. Some might even try to wear it as a badge of honor, constantly talking about their busy life. However, this is not the way to run a productive business.

Being busy reduces your productivity, keeps you from focusing on things that really matter, and leads to working hard while serving your clients less. If you're wondering what a busy person looks like compared to a productive person, here are some characteristics:

MULTI-MILLION DOLLAR PRODUCTIVITY FORMULA

CHARACTERISTICS OF A BUSY PERSON

- Multitasking
- Saying yes to too many things
- Working harder
- Driven by stress
- Easily distracted
- Never on time
- Often behind on tasks

VS

CHARACTERISTICS OF A PRODUCTIVE PERSON

- Never rushed
- Plan in advance
- Never late
- Relaxed
- Utilize tools and strategies
- Driven by purpose, vision, mission, and passion
- Start the day with things that infuse purpose
- Able to say no
- Put their well-being first
- Set and achieve high expectations
- Do deep work
- Work smart
- Focus on how to better serve their ideal clients
- Know their agenda for the year, quarter, month, week, and day

HOW TO BECOME A PRODUCTIVE BUSINESS OWNER

To become productive, you must learn one primary skill: saying no. People who are busy, frantic, and ineffective tend to say yes to too many things. Saying yes to everything is a clear path to destruction because it takes us away from who we are and what we are called to do.

Productivity is about actively producing quality products and services that align with your vision and purpose. It's not about being busy. God created us to produce incredible things to bring positive change to our world. We must align with our purpose and seek the proper steps to deliver services that make an impact.

You were never intended to do everything for everybody. The decisions you make are critical and need to be guided by this vital principle:

Every yes you say that does not align with your purpose and mission is a no to you.

- It is a no to your mission.
- It is a no to your purpose.
- It is a no to the calling within you.

I will only say yes to you if it is also a yes to me. That may sound selfish, but it is not. Putting yourself first is the right thing to do for this important reason: Service comes from a place of abundance. If you are going to do your best for your business, employees, clients, community, and world, you will need to serve out of that abundance. When you say yes to things not aligned with your purpose, you will soon be operating from a place of lack.

It may be out of your comfort zone if you are not accustomed to thinking this way. If you have the habit of always saying yes, it may take some practice to learn the skill of saying no. So let me help.

When you are faced with a decision, there is a simple checklist that you can use to see if it aligns with what you do as a business owner. In every aspect of your day, ask yourself if your activity does at least one of the following:

- Produce money
- Save money
- Save time
- Produce impact
- Improve systems and processes

When you serve your customers, you are making money. When you take steps to run your office efficiently, you save money. With every decision and activity, check to see if it meets the criteria on this list. If it doesn't, it is time to say no.

Here is an example of an activity that easily meets the criteria. Every Thursday, I have a meeting with my staff. The purpose of this meeting is to discuss the clients' journey and make improvements. Our focus is on how we can enhance the clients' experience and further automate our processes.

For example, when clients come into our practice, they receive automated emails to move them to the next steps. This enables the client to have a seamless experience moving from their decision to contact our office to getting an appointment and moving through their journey. We automate the communication process as much as possible so that nothing gets overlooked and the client has the best experience.

Focusing on automation and ways to improve our process also saves money because my administrative staff spends less hands-on time on these tasks. Therefore, this weekly meeting improves our processes and systems, impacts the client, and saves money. Ultimately, this impact on the client increases referrals, producing more money and more opportunities to impact lives.

This is a meeting that needs a yes. Imagine a scenario where a business owner is too rushed, overwhelmed, or disorganized to have this type of regularly scheduled meeting with this kind of focus.

The staff remains stuck in ineffective practices without automation. As a result, the client's experience is negatively affected, and both time and money are wasted. All of this is because they didn't have time for a weekly meeting. In reality, it is a cop-out to say there was no time. Everyone has the same twenty-four-hour day. The question is how you choose to use those hours.

Productive business owners who use their time wisely and say yes only to things that meet their criteria find themselves working less, with less stress and more results. This is the goal.

TOOLS FOR THE JOB

When you are productive in your life and business, you know your strengths, growth areas, and ideal clients. You only say yes to things that align with your purpose. You work productively and feel empowered by your work. Finally, let's look at some simple tools and practices that can help increase your focus.

Use a timer. I always use a timer to keep me focused on the task at hand. Never jump from task to task. Never multitask, and don't let your mind drift. Schedule a time to work on a task and set a timer. During that time, focus only on that task. Set a realistic amount of time to complete a task or one element of a task, and then get it done. This is how to check things off your list and feel good about your accomplishments for the day.

Set a place to work. We are all creatures of habit. When you train yourself to work in a particular space, your mind automatically goes into work mode when you sit there. Keep it free from distractions and have everything you need for your tasks readily available. You don't want to be working on your laptop only to find that it is not charged and you can't find your charger. Have a place to work where your charger and other such items are accessible, and you can focus on your task.

Use a planner. There are many types of planners available to keep you organized. Everything from a basic paper calendar to a phone calendar or an executive planner can work. Find what works for you. Everyone has their own preferences, but there are a few things to keep in mind. You need easy access to more than your daily schedule.

Remember, your daily schedule is set by your yearly, quarterly, monthly, and weekly goals based on your purpose, vision, and mission. All of these need to be easily accessed in your planner so that these goals continue to guide your daily activities.

By following these principles, you will be empowered in your work, focused on your goals, and living your purpose. You can leave behind the days of being busy, stressed, and frustrated. You will be more efficient, less stressed, on time, and better able to serve your clients. Plus, your clients, employees, contractors, community, and family will all benefit from your new levels of productivity. Through productivity, you will be a happier, healthier, and wealthier business owner. This is what you were called to be.

CHAPTER TAKEAWAYS

- Busy people are exhausted, burned out, and unable to focus on their goals.
- Productive people are energized, focused, and feel empowered to tackle their days.

- The difference between busy and productive is planning, structure, and alignment with your purpose.
- Finding tools that help you be productive instead of busy will profoundly impact your life and business.

Chapter 9

Dominate the Market, Reproduce and Distribute

In previous chapters, we've discussed creating a healthy relationship with money and the importance of being productive as a business owner. Now, let's dive into how we use productivity to make money and how making money increases our impact and helps us fulfill our purpose in our market.

Dominating the market is not about financial gain—although that's usually a side effect of what I'm going to ask of you in this chapter. This chapter is about becoming the go-to expert in your field. It's about picking a specialty or a niche and zeroing in on those skills so that your competition is no longer a concern. You will be so good at what you do that no one else even comes close.

When I started SMPsychotherapy I knew I needed to use my gifts. My areas of strength as a therapist provided the path, but I also did some market research to figure out how to best market my gifts. I excel at therapy that empowers women to take action. Talking about mental health is important, but unless we take action we don't see any real changes. My gift as a therapist is to help people develop skills so they don't need to keep coming to see me week after week. My market research indicates that women are the decision makers about mental healthcare in their families.

To dominate the market, I needed to focus on the action needed to improve mental health, and market to women and their families. Sure, we treat children, men, and nonbinary folk as well, but we market to women because that's the best avenue for connecting people with our services.

What is your specialty? What therapy superpower makes you stand out from other clinicians? That's your niche. Don't be afraid to be different; being like everyone else is boring. Find what makes you unique, and use that to create your business. What is your specialty?

Once I had my therapy specialty nailed down, I was ready to reproduce my services. To understand the importance of reproducing services, we need to first understand that God created us to take possession of the earth and do amazing work while we are here.

God created us to produce, but He also wants us to help humankind as much as possible. As medical professionals, therapists, etc., the more clients we can help reach their potential, the more aligned we are with our purpose. You were created to produce amazing things and then to offer them to as many people in need as possible. In the previous chapter, we discussed productivity. Productivity is about actively producing quality products and services that align with your vision and purpose. Once you have your products and services, you need to replicate them to extend your impact.

With the right tools, private practice owners can create a business model that supports the volume distribution of products and services. This gives us a greater impact on the world and a better chance of building the financial freedom we want when we start our entrepreneurial journey. Successful business owners decide quickly to move forward with an action plan to achieve their vision. We don't hide our gifts. We use them to produce something that impacts the world.

In 2018 when I started my private practice, I envisioned working part-time as a solo provider while keeping my job in the school district. When my robust marketing strategy yielded a long wait-list, I knew I needed to find a way to reproduce my services so I could impact more lives.

This realization prompted me to do an SGOT analysis related to changing my business model. My strength is that I have a strong business mindset, and I am business savvy, and I had my MBA learning to fall back on. I had confidence because I continuously worked on my mindset. My growth areas were that I was playing too small, that I didn't have the time I needed to see more clients. The threat to succeeding in meeting the needs of potential clients by replicating my services was staying in my job, not having an office space, and being limited by my personal schedule.

I decided to create a plan to serve more clients. First, I addressed the time constraints by quitting my job with the school district and going full-time in private practice. Next, I rented an office space on a per-session basis. Then, I hired additional therapists who shared my mission and vision. These decisions allowed me to replicate my services and expand SMPsychotherapy.

Let's take a broader view of mental health care needs. According to the World Health Organization, more than eighty percent of people with mental health conditions do not have access to adequate care.[2] People struggling with mental health conditions are more likely to suffer physical ailments, be disabled, experience human rights violations, and face early death.[3] Mental health suffering costs the global economy over $1 trillion USD per calendar year.

There is demand for your services. There is a larger need for your services that you can meet as an individual therapist.

Reproducing your services is about not hiding your gifts, talents, and abilities from the world, but sharing them. It's a disservice to the world to take our genius to the grave. We have a responsibility to use our gifts and abilities to produce something massive that shifts the world and the energy of the next generation into a more positive space than it was when we started.

2   Ghebreyesus, T. A. (2019). *The WHO Special Initiative for Mental Health (2019–2023): Universal Health Coverage for Mental Health*. World Health Organization. http://www.jstor.org/stable/resrep28223.

3   ibid

MULTI-MILLION DOLLAR SERVICE REPRODUCTION FORMULA

YOUR PROFIT INCREASES WHEN YOU REPRODUCE YOUR SERVICES

SOLO PROVIDER

* You have 30 hours available to meet with clients each week.

* Insurance reimbursement rate is $100 per hour.

* Your calendar is full, the most you can hope to make in a week is $3,000.

* Subtract your overhead costs for payroll, accounting, office space, insurance, etc. and you're earning less.

* You might be able to afford the basic necessities for you and your family with that income, but what if you could do more?

VS

GROUP PRACTICE

* You are running a group practice employing 20 therapists who can all see 30 clients each week.

* You keep a portion of the insurance reimbursement rates for the business and the therapist keeps a portion.

* Your business can now service 600 clients each week, offers employment opportunities, and makes 20 times as much revenue.

* Now, consider your financial situation if you add in online courses, books, speaking engagements and other ways to broaden your reach.

Reproducing your services is the most direct path to achieving your purpose on Earth. God created you to do amazing work here on Earth. He didn't create you to wait until you get to heaven to fulfill your purpose. It's time to get to work and fulfill your purpose while you're here. How do we serve the masses? How do we impact more people?

We have to create a business model that supports expansion and replication. Then, we have to offer the same or similar services over and over again. Think of a large corporation with franchises all over the world. Any corporation will do this exercise. Consider the services and products offered by that company. Are they the same across all franchises? Are there differences in products and services depending on where a franchise office is located? How does franchising allow that company to grow and create a larger impact on the world?

In the same way, a franchise differs from location to location. If you hire additional therapists, they may work in a slightly different way than you. They may have a different specialty, or they may use different methods. As long as their goal for impact on the world aligns with your company mission and vision, trust them to do the work. Allow people the opportunity to fulfill their own purpose, support their family, and increase the impact of your company as a whole.

Let's talk for a moment about the way your profit increases when you reproduce your services. As a private practice therapist, without reproduction of services your income is limited by the number of clients you meet with each week. If you have thirty hours available to meet with clients each week, the insurance reimbursement rate is one hundred dollars per hour, and your calendar is full, the most you can hope to make in a week is $3,000. Now, subtract your overhead costs for payroll, accounting, office space, insurance, etc. and you're earning less. Sure, you might be able to afford the basic necessities for you and your family with that income, but what if you could do more?

Now, imagine you are running a group practice employing twenty therapists who can all see thirty clients each week. You keep a portion of the insurance reimbursement rates for the business and the therapist keeps a portion. Your business can now service 600 clients each week, offer employment opportunities, and make twenty times as much revenue. Now, consider your financial situation if you add in online courses, books, speaking engagements and other ways to broaden your reach.

You are a mental health professional. You are in the business of helping others realize and meet their potential. Imagine if you could reach two, three, or twenty times as many people with your unique skills. Could you do more?

I felt called to do more. In 2013, I found myself lying on a table in a doctor's office, an ultrasound wand on my swollen abdomen, and my young son, John Anthony, reading a book in the corner. He'd been to countless doctor's appointments with me after thirty-six weeks of pregnancy, and he learned to tune out the sound of the heartbeat whooshing over the speaker.

This time, though, there was no heartbeat. My tiny little salsa dancer wasn't moving. His heart no longer beat, and I suddenly had to find a way to mother my son while saying goodbye to the son I never got to hold. In the coming months, I'd bury my son, return all the baby equipment I purchased, and find a way to move forward.

In all that time, I never asked God why he took my son. I knew the answer wasn't something that would bring me peace or make the next months and years of my life easier. Sometimes there is no reason for loss. But, no matter how profound our grief, we can choose to wallow in it, or channel it into something greater.

Sure, I spent some time wallowing; honoring your emotions is the best way forward. But then, I decided to find purpose in my grief. What does this story have to do with reproducing goods and services to maximize profit?

Let me explain. Massive profit allows you to make a massive impact on the world. In honor of Jean Carlos, my tiny salsa dancer, I started JC's Precious Minds Foundation. This nonprofit serves single mothers raising special needs children in the Dominican Republic. As a Dominican woman, I am intimately familiar with the education system in my home country, and I understand the struggle parents of special needs children have getting their little ones the services they need to thrive. The revenue produced by SMPSychotherapy allowed me to start this foundation, which has since qualified for grants and outside funding, which allowed us to grow our organization and expand our reach. Now, we not only provide services to the youngsters, but education and business coaching to their mothers so they are able to support their families for generations to come.

This is what taking possession of the earth means. God created us to build legacies of success that impact future generations and make this world better. Do you have a clear understanding of the potential you hold? Dream a bit—what do you want? What is your purpose? Do you wish to decrease poverty, improve mental health outcomes, empower women, reduce food insecurity? What impact do you want to have on the world?

You need money to make that happen, and reproducing your services so you can reach more people is how you fulfill your purpose. Distributing those services is your insurance policy. Distribution ensures that your reproduced products and services get to the people who need them and have the impact you intended from the onset.

When I talk about distribution, I often mention words like expansion and marketing. Often, thanks to profit-centered human-exploiting businesses, those words have a negative connotation. Let's reframe that using a story from my early days as a private practice owner.

When I started working individually, I felt rushed to get people results because that was the mindset in agencies and in the school system. If you've worked in agencies, you probably have some of the same tendencies. You're focused on numbers, efficiency, and output. Let's get rid of that thinking. What if you could spend however long you deemed necessary with clients? What if you could help them find real, sustainable results that improve their lives long after they leave your therapy office? What if you could develop a model where you're helping people find long-term relief from the problems that brought them to therapy in the first place? What if you could serve clients at a high level, invest time and resources into their care, and truly live your purpose?

If these questions excite you as a private practice owner, you're ready to discuss distribution. Distribution simply means getting the services you created and reproduced for your ideal client into the hands of as many people who fit that avatar as possible.

Distributing your services requires a few things: long-term business planning, keeping your customer in mind, and having a clear business model. I discuss more on each of these pieces in the coming chapters, so I won't repeat them here. I will give you an overview of each requirement for distribution so you can start dreaming bigger.

Long-term business planning allows you to think strategically about your goals and make conscious choices that impact not just today, but your future. I urge clients to set goals at intervals of one month, three months, six months, one year, three years, and five years. If you're only planning for short-term growth you're living in triage mode rather than thinking strategically.

Keeping your customer in mind is key to any marketing decision you make. This is more than just identifying the demographics of your ideal client. Think about the problems they have that you're uniquely qualified to solve. How do they feel about their life? How would they like to feel instead? Market surveys and polling existing clients will help you set those long-term business goals to ensure you're providing exactly what your customers need at every stage of your business.

A clear business model can help you decide if you need to focus on serving consumers or other businesses. When I first started, I only served customers. Now that I've found success, I serve both customers and other businesses. Understanding what your business does will help you make decisions in alignment with your mission and vision.

Part three of this book will walk you through how to make decisions about what services to offer, and help you plan for replication and distribution, so you can dominate the market, create a massive impact on the world, and create the life and business of your dreams. Take a deep breath, turn the page, and get ready to dive into the Multi-Million-Dollar Private Practice Framework™.

CHAPTER TAKEAWAYS

- Dominating the market requires you to specialize.
- Specializing allows you to narrow in on your ideal client, products, and services that solve the problems they deal with, and know you're providing high value.
- Once you've specialized, you must find a way to reproduce your goods and services.
- Reproduction allows you to impact more people and increase profit.
- Distributing your services widely via marketing efforts, online courses, books, and other means guarantees longevity, profitability, and impact.

Part 3

The Multi-Million-Dollar Private Practice Framework™

The rest of this book contains absolute gold. This section outlines the eight pillars of The Multi-Million-Dollar Private Practice Framework I developed to build and scale my business. SMPsychotherapy and Counseling Services started as a solo practice operating on evenings and weekends around my "real job"—until I realized that job that seemed stable and safe was neither. By using the principles outlined here, I grew SMPsychotherapy into a thriving practice employing over twenty therapists, several medical providers, and countless support staff. We serve over 11,000 clients in Connecticut and are currently expanding to Massachusetts and New York. This year, my practice is set to make over 250 million dollars in revenue after only four years in business. Let me show you how you can build your own profitable, impactful business.

Chapter 10

Multi-Million-Dollar Business Mindset Formula™

Often, when I speak with helping professionals in private practice, they tell me that regular business principles don't apply to them because they are in the business of serving and helping others. They aren't just in it to make a profit.

I differ because I view the business of providing services is the highest form of helping others. When you run a business that heals and helps others grow, you are not practicing. You are running a business. You are in the business of impacting and transforming lives. You are in the business of providing opportunities to other helping professionals. You are in the business of leading others and creating a legacy of change. You are a business person running a business. You aren't practicing.

A business is created in collaboration with God and others who can see your vision and are willing to support it. All of the tools we discussed in parts one and two are vital to your success. You must know exactly what you want your business to do, then you have to work to align your purpose, vision, and mission. You'll need to develop the skills to manage your thoughts and emotions as business takes off and as it struggles. You'll need to constantly connect to your why to develop new products and services that help you meet the needs of your clients in new ways.

To do all of that, you need a business mindset. This is the first of our Multi-Million-Dollar Private Practice Framework™. In Chapter 3, we discuss the importance of learning to manage your thoughts and emotions as a leader. In this chapter, we will apply those principles directly to business.

A business mindset says that you can manage your thoughts and emotions in relation to your business. You can weigh the benefits and costs of every decision and count on the decisions you make being the right ones for you and everyone who works for and is connected with your organization. You know you can learn and grow as a business owner and create a workplace and service that meets the needs of all stakeholders.

In March 2020, I was on my way home from vacation with my son. When my plane landed, I got alerts about the country shutting down due to the COVID-19 pandemic. I sat in the seat as others deplaned, my son next to me, and I frantically read the guidelines. There was no way I could continue business as usual.

At that point, my practice offered in-home therapy to most of our clients and saw a few in an office space we rented on a per session basis. If I couldn't see my clients, I wouldn't be able to submit to their insurance companies, and my entire livelihood would crash.

My choices at that moment were to fight against the wave of panic, or give in to it and let my business and my dreams crumble. When I decided to start a business, though, I decided to continuously fight for growth, improvement, and innovation.

I looked into my business networks and saw desperation, hopelessness, and an overwhelming sense of loss.

How can I keep my practice going?

How will my practice survive if we can't see clients?

What will we do when we can't pay our bills?

These people were running a practice, not a business. I was running a business that happened to be a group therapy practice. A business looks at the market and pivots based on trends and client needs. A business analyzes results and pushes through obstacles. I needed to pivot, analyze, and push.

In part one of this book, we did plenty of self-analysis to determine personal areas of strength and growth. In business, we call it a SGOT analysis. Whatever you call it, the process is the same.

As always, this process began with evaluating my current situation. I had no control over the pandemic, or the shutdown of in-person service that resulted from it. I completed an instant SGOT analysis to identify barriers to success and areas of growth for my business. Then I decided that the only real option was to teach my clients to use Telehealth services.

Then the next day I took off my vacation hat and became a technology trainer. I walked each client through how to use the online platforms available so that when the time came, they didn't miss a single appointment.

In business, your SGOT analysis will go something like this:

Where am I right now?

My business was successful and profitable with the in-person therapy offered in home or in a rented office space. My clients were happy with the model, and it worked for me. However, the pandemic was something out of my control that impacted my ability to continue business as usual. I needed to learn as much as possible about the pandemic and how we expected it to impact the world of mental health.

I had to make a decision.

I needed to decide to fight through the pandemic, or let an unexpected world-wide phenomenon decide if my business was successful or not. I decided not to let the pandemic destroy my business. I was going to find a way to pivot.

I called on my support system.

From the beginning, my business had the support of an accountant, a billing department, and administrative staff. The work of these professionals allowed me to focus on my area of genius and maximize my impact. I let them know of the changes I was making to our business model, and let them worry about how their roles fit into those changes.

When you have the right support system, you can have faith that they will be willing to do their best work for you, and confidence that they can handle any situation.

I reviewed my purpose, vision, and mission. I'll discuss these in more detail in the chapter on business planning, but here's an overview of how they interact.

My purpose guides every decision I make in my personal and professional life. Working in alignment is the path to success. In situations where you must adapt or fail, staying in alignment ensures that you adapt because failing to provide what your clients need will not help you fulfill your purpose. My purpose is to help others heal and transform their lives.

My vision is my long-term goal for SMPsychotherapy and how I want the organization to impact the world.

My mission, or the way I reached my vision and purpose, is what needed to change to adapt to the pandemic. Instead of reaching clients' needs through in-home or in-office therapy, I needed to adapt to the need for Telehealth.

I invited in a new perspective.

Our perspective of a situation affects the thoughts and emotions we have about it. When I spoke with my colleagues in March 2020, the prevailing perspectives were somewhere between despair and denial. Many providers feared they wouldn't be able to adapt their business to the changing needs of the world, while others felt the pandemic would be over in a matter of weeks.

Discussions of how this isolation might impact mental health were just starting to gain traction, and I knew providers needed to prepare themselves for the long haul. People were going to need healthcare services now more than ever. I needed to pray, meditate, and be open to the perspective that our business would prevail. I could still connect with clients. I could still develop therapeutic relationships. I could learn to use Telehealth.

I took inspired, massive action.

Making a decision and inviting in a new perspective isn't helpful if we don't act. Once I decided to move forward, whether it was with getting my professional license in 2018, pivoting to Telehealth in 2020, or adding medication management services in 2021, I first committed to an inspired action that would shift my momentum.

Once I took the first step of signing up for video conferencing services, the rest fell into place. Inspired action leads to massive action and massive action will take you around any roadblock.

In March 2020, I spent an entire day teaching clients how to access Zoom. I hired a service coordinator and therapists who were willing to provide online therapy. I did not lose money. In fact, this shift to Telehealth is one of the practices that led SMPsychotherapy to have its first million-dollar year.

I set goals, then I revised them.

Initially, my goal was to provide in-home or in-office therapy as a solo provider. Then, I transitioned to group practice. When the pandemic threatened to interrupt services, I pivoted again and created new goals.

A business mindset is a growth mindset on steroids.

If you're starting a business for the first time, you may not have the skills to adjust and pivot when a new challenge presents itself in your business. I work with my coaching clients on developing a business mindset using the following formula. To begin with, we write it out as an exercise every time we have a big decision to make for the business. With enough practice, managing your mindset to be one of growth, strength, and success becomes second nature.

MULTI-MILLION-DOLLAR BUSINESS MINDSET FORMULA™

Align your purpose, vision, and mission and ensure every decision you make will help all three. If you take only one thing away from this book, I hope it's the idea of alignment and how it's more important than any other piece of this business mindset and business strategy work. Alignment ensures you feel energized by your business, not shackled by it.

Identify your desires for your business. What do you really want your business to accomplish this week, this month, this quarter, this year, and in three to five years?

This is the step in creating a business mindset where imposter syndrome is most likely to creep in. You start dreaming about what you want for your business and BAM! A little voice creeps in telling you that you can't have it for some reason or another.

Imposter syndrome is that voice that tells you all the things you cannot do, have, or be. It tells you that you aren't good enough, smart enough, or brave enough to have the business and life you want.

But you also get something out of letting imposter syndrome take over. Imposter syndrome is a story you tell yourself so you don't have to stretch outside your comfort zone. When you give into imposter syndrome it reaffirms what you already believe about yourself. Maybe you heard from others you weren't good enough, you aren't qualified, and are constantly chasing that reinforcement the imposter syndrome reaffirms your negative, limiting beliefs.

Alice, a business coaching client of mine, resettles imposter syndrome any time we introduce something new for her business. Each new product or service she decides to launch leads to her questioning her skills, talents, and accomplishments. She wrestles with the idea that she's not equipped to do what she wants to do, even though she is objectively qualified.

A few months ago, we introduced the idea of a show on social media via Facebook live. The show would feature her and her family using produce from their community farm to create healthy delicious meals. She does this all the time with her family, but she is doubtful and scared of putting it out on social media.

The work we do together when imposter syndrome takes over is the dirty chair process from Chapter 3. We crush imposter syndrome by assessing where she is, what she's feeling, thinking, and how it's holding her back. I want you to do the same thing when imposter syndrome threatens you.

What are the mindset issues that tell you that you can't do this new thing? What experiences have told you that you aren't good enough? Where did you learn that you don't deserve this next level of success?

Then tell imposter syndrome to shut up and decide to shift the story.

Journal and talk about how you are going to shift the story, and what actions you will take to build confidence. Remember, confidence requires repeated, successful action. Remind yourself of all the things you've done to date, and all the ways you've experienced success. Then create a mantra to repeat every time imposter syndrome tries to bubble up.

1. How do your desires align with the impact you want to create in your community? Who are you helping? How does the success you want for your business impact the community you decided to serve?

2. How do you want to feel working in your business and working on your business? What sort of culture do you want to create? Employees, customers, clients, and other stakeholders will have the same experience working and enjoying your services as you have creating them.

3. How would you behave as a business owner and leader in your community? What is your identity? Who do you want to be? What qualities do you need to embody? What work do you need to do to become that person?

4. Describe your behaviors as a successful private practice business owner: what are some of the inspired steps you take? A person with a business mindset is constantly working to become who they want to be in their personal life and in business.

Think of the people you can partner with, services, books, and courses you can use to develop those skills. This personal and professional development goes beyond continuing education units

(CEUs) and encompasses therapy, business coaching, life coaching, conferences, courses, books, mentors, and other partnerships.

As therapists, medical providers, and helping professionals, we often struggle with business mindset. We undervalue our time, underpay ourselves, and struggle to shift that mindset. If you're still not sure that a business mindset is the ticket to success for you, look at this perspective. Being in business is the business of service and helping. Providing our services, marketing. and connecting to the people who need our services is vital; without your business the world misses out on your gifts.

Business mindset is the highest form of helper mindset. Don't let people miss out on your gifts because you're afraid to lean in.

Not that long ago, a colleague of mine who owns a private practice called me for medication management for an uninsured patient. I quoted our standard price for medication management appointments with a highly qualified APRN. My colleague was upset. He said I'm overcharging for the services.

SMPsychotherapy has a grant that offers help to the community, but we did not have funds at the time. We help undocumented, uninsured, and homeless families through that grant. We cannot extend that to everyone, otherwise we cannot pay our employees. As business owners, we cannot think of helping as giving things for free or low cost. Our business model must produce revenue and profit. We can have availability to help those in need, but we cannot ONLY do that.

You will also encounter people in helping professions who balk at your prices or tell you that charging for your services is not the "right" thing to do. When people say these things to you, be clear, be aligned with your vision, mission, and purpose. The best way to show people that you can be successful while adhering to your purpose and having a positive impact is to just keep doing it.

Without a business mindset, you will fail. Your private practice will go under. If you are running a business without profit, you are running a nonprofit. You can help, you can serve, you can offer charity, but businesses must generate money, or it's just a hobby.

You want to change the world? You need money to change the world. Money is energy, and energy is how we make change. Change the world, but be profitable first.

A business mindset is the basis for all of your business growth. Without the right mindset, you will continue to spin your wheels, have trouble making decisions, and hold yourself back from the impact and financial success you want.

Cultivating a business mindset is not something that happens overnight. Just as cultivating a garden takes time for initial setup as well as careful weeding, pruning, and watering, your mindset will require maintenance. Maintenance can come from coaching, connecting with other business professionals, self-development books, and more.

For more personalized support with your business mindset, I invite you to take The Multi-Million-Dollar Business Mindset Assessment. This assessment includes a one-on-one session with me and a detailed plan to address any mindset issues holding you back from creating the life and business of your dreams.

BOOK YOUR MINDSET ASSESSMENT

Even though you will need to work on your mindset continuously, do not wait to move on to the next step. Business planning is coming up next, and the momentum you build as you plan and build your business will help to reinforce all the mindset work you do. So, work on your mindset while building your business with the Multi-Million-Dollar Private Practice Framework™. Don't wait. Turn the page and jump into creating your business plan.

CHAPTER TAKEAWAYS

- Alignment is the first step in developing a business mindset.
- Tuning out external noise and identifying your desires is vital to fulfilling your purpose.
- Imposter syndrome is real, and will try to steal your success. Learning to identify when it pops up and how to manage it will help ensure your success.
- A business mindset will allow you to share your gifts with the world.

Chapter 11

Multi-Million-Dollar Business Plan Framework™

The first Pillar of Private Practice is your mindset, and it is the foundation of your entrepreneurial journey. Once you have a foundation laid, you need a plan to build the rest. That brings us to our second pillar, business planning.

When I first started my business in 2018, my plan was to run a solo practice. I was going to provide services on my own in home settings, or in a rented office space. At the time, I had no funding so an office I could use for twenty dollars per session seemed like my best bet.

I'd keep my day-job as a school social worker and work on the weekends and in the evenings. I thought it was important to keep my medical benefits as I built a business.

I wrote a business plan complete with a purpose statement, a vision, and a mission. I detailed my business model, decided on my ideal clients and the services I would offer. I started a limited liability company and started marketing. I wrote goals for my first year, and three years out. My goals described how many clients I wanted to have, how much revenue I wanted to make, and who I would hire along the way.

My business plan was comprehensive, well-written, and stated exactly how I was going to build a Queendom.

It took me longer to write this business plan than the document lasted.

The demand for my services was bigger than I could have imagined. My marketing efforts filled my open appointments and my waitlist, and it became apparent that I needed to change my plan—quickly.

My purpose is to help as many people as possible achieve their dreams and create the lives they want. I cannot possibly do that if I'm working on evenings and weekends with a waitlist longer than the flight to my dream vacation in Dubai.

My waitlist was too long.

I used an SGOT analysis to identify my current strengths, growth areas, and opportunities for growth, as well as the possible threats to my business. I realized that my business plan was out of alignment with my vision. My vision was big, but I was working small. At that time, I was reinvesting most of what I made back into my business.

I didn't have the money, because I didn't have the time.

I was playing small.

I decided to adjust my business plan. My business plan needs to be in alignment with my vision, purpose, and mission. I decided to quit my job and go full time as a private practice owner.

Even though I didn't use that first business plan long, I'm glad I wrote it because it showed me I was playing too small. I was working for someone else and fulfilling their dream when I had the capacity to quit right then. A business plan organized my knowledge and thoughts and that organization pushed me to confront my fears.

If your business mindset is the foundation of your entrepreneurial journey, and organized knowledge propels you forward, then a business plan is the blueprint for the entire structure. Creating a business plan requires you to make decisions about every aspect of your business.

These decisions are essential, but they are not permanent. You can change your business plan at any time as you grow and learn. You want your business plan to change because your SGOT analysis will point out opportunities for growth and improvement. SMPsychotherapy has been in business for four and a half years. I've reviewed and updated my business plan twenty-one times.

Many times, when I coach people, they worry about changing their business plan or take a long time to make decisions. I encourage all business owners to make decisions quickly based on data and analysis. Eventually, business owners grow to like the change—maybe even crave it. I like the constant change in my business because it gives me a sense of purpose and a sense that I am in control of my future. I am in control of how I'm moving this business forward.

So, how do you write a comprehensive business plan that is a living, changing document? Let's detail the components of a successful plan.

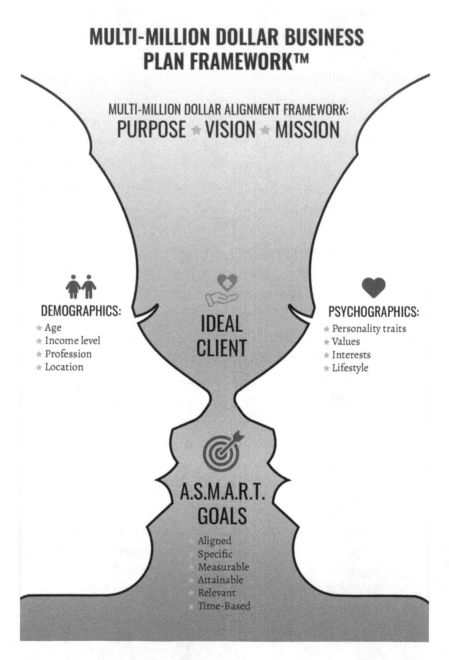

PURPOSE, VISION, MISSION

Your business plan should include your mission statement and vision. Our plans will also include a statement of purpose. A vision includes your current and future objectives. The mission includes a description of the business and how you plan to serve your clients. The mission and vision serve as a guidepost pointing you and any employees you have in the direction of success. They also help potential clients determine if you're the right company for them.

PURPOSE

Your purpose is why you are here. It's the reason God created you, your motivation.

My purpose statement:

My purpose in life is to have freedom in all areas of my life and teach others around the world to do the same. I want to live and work in an environment that promotes peace, creativity, harmony, so I can be of greater service to my family, my community, and the world at large. In this current phase of my life, my purpose is to help others build a queendom legacy that allows them to build an unbreakable life, career, and business. My purpose at this point is so ingrained in me that it's all I see. Everything I do is in alignment with this purpose. People feel comfortable working for me. Because of the peace and harmony, they feel free to invent and be creative. I got here by visualizing how myself and others would feel in my space.

VISION

Your vision is what you're meant to do and what impact you want to have on the world.

My vision statement:

My vision is to create a queendom legacy that extends beyond me to the future generations. My company will change the lives of individuals, families, and communities. I want people to use the skills and strategies we teach them to build their own queendom legacy. My vision is to give people tools so they can replicate them again and again and teach them to future generations. I do this by honoring my ancestors and fulfilling their dreams for me.

MISSION

Your mission is how you fulfill your purpose and vision. It's the tiny steps along the path to your vision.

My mission statement.

I will expand SMPsychotherapy to serve people, families, and communities in every city in the US, by writing books that can inspire others to create their own queendom legacy, to write stories so people can see themselves, to speak so my word can motivate others to reclaim the power in their own voice, to provide services that will transform lives so others can create a legacy that transcends their own vision. I do this through therapy work, books, public speaking, and philanthropy work with JC's Precious Minds Foundation.

Of the three, your mission is most likely to change. As your company grows, the way you do business and the steps you take will change to help you reach your vision, and ultimately your purpose.

IDEAL CLIENTS

In your business plan, take time to detail your ideal clients or customers. Include demographics such as age, income level, profession, and location, but don't stop there. Detail your ideal clients' emotions and the problems your services and products can help them solve.

I create an ideal client avatar—a fake person who is the perfect client for our practice. The market we serve is women and families. This sometimes makes people think we don't serve men. We do. But women are often the head of making decisions about the mental health and wellness services their families need. So, my business plan targets women, and then their families through them. The ideal client influences your marketing plan, which we discuss in Chapter 15, your hiring plan you'll create in Chapter 17, and many other areas of your business plan.

GOAL-SETTING

A business plan contains short and long-term goals. The goals should center on financials, client impact, community impact, and services. Fight the urge to set small goals. I select goals for my business that stretch me outside my comfort zone. If you know you can achieve your goals without difficulty, there is no challenge there. I want a goal that scares me; if it doesn't scare me, it doesn't make sense to tackle it.

Your business plan must also include goals for your business. Make your goals ASMART: Aligned, Specific, Measurable, Achievable, Realistic, and Time-Based. Having goals for one, three, six, twelve-month and five-year intervals is also a great idea.

- Aligned goals keep your purpose, vision, and mission in mind. A goal that doesn't support the reason you do the work you do will not help your life and business long term.

- Specific: Rather, than "I will fill my caseload," try "I will serve twenty clients." Being specific allows for better reflection on goal achievement and planning for the future.
- Measurable: Your goal should include a measurable outcome. In the statement, "I will serve twenty clients," adding "each week" makes it easier to measure success. If you're only serving fifteen clients a week, but have twenty clients total, you've not met your goal yet.
- Attainable: Your goal should fit into the time constraints without taking away from the time you need to complete back-office tasks. If you only have time for fifteen clients a week when you account for office work and your personal life, set your goal accordingly!
- Relevant: Your goals should relate directly to your mission and vision. If the goal doesn't fit into your long-term plans—get rid of it! You don't have time for distracting dribs and drabs as a business owner.
- Time-Based: Stating that you want to serve twenty clients a week is great, but in long-term planning, you want to set goals with an end date in mind to help you adjust marketing efforts, set up systems and processes, etc. "I will serve twenty clients a week within six months of opening my business" is a long-term goal that will allow you to track progress, adjust your efforts, and reflect as you go.

VISION BOARD FOR GOAL-SETTING

For me, there is a heavy spiritual component to goal-setting. In 2021, I visited the Palace Theater in Waterbury, CT to listen to a speaker. They walked across the stage, commanding the audience and speaking about purpose, why we were created, and spirituality. Sitting there with my friend and event coordinator, I felt this transcendental experience where I was the speaker and speaking to a room full of people. It lasted a second, and then it was gone. I tapped my friend on the shoulder and whispered about my experience.

"I felt the same thing."

"We have to come to the Palace Theater."

I now have a goal to bring Unbreakable at the Palace theater in Waterbury with a crowd of 600 or more people. Making that decision scared me. I've done plenty of small events, but an event of over 600 scares me.

I create a step-by-step plan by activating my inner GPS: where is my business now, where do I want to go? I'm adding more and more speaking engagements to my calendar in alignment with the goal of increasing the impact of my coaching business. I mapped out the plan step by step. My goals are always time-bound, because I want to know my destination and when I plan to get there.

So, I booked the Palace for October 2024.

Sometimes, my deadline approaches and I've yet to accomplish my goal. I can see that it's not going to happen this time. So, I return to my SGOT analysis, adjust my plan, and set a new timeline based on where I am now.

This will happen to you, too, if you accomplish every goal you set in the timeframe you set, you are playing too small. Big impact from a purpose-driven business requires massive goals with aggressive timelines.

When you have a business mindset, missing the deadline for your goal is not a time to beat yourself up or let imposter syndrome take over. It's not a time to settle into that dirty chair. It's time to practice self-compassion, assessment, and redirecting.

BUSINESS PLANNING WITH THE MULTI-MILLION-DOLLAR PRIVATE PRACTICE FRAMEWORK™

In addition to your purpose, vision, and mission statements, ideal client, and goal setting, your business plan will contain detailed information about your business model, your business structure, marketing plan, team building practices, and personal and professional development, and systems and supports to keep your business running smoothly. We discuss each of these components in the coming chapters. They make up the remaining Pillars of Private Practice. I can't wait to see the plan you create and the business you build.

CHAPTER TAKEAWAYS

- The most important piece of business planning is ensuring you have alignment with your purpose, vision, and mission.
- Your purpose, vision and mission will guide you toward effective goal setting.
- Goals must be ASMART: Aligned, Specific, Measurable, Achievable, Realistic, and Time-based in order to be effective.
- When setting goals, it's important to keep in mind who you need to become in order to achieve what you want to achieve.

Chapter 12

Multi-Million-Dollar Business Models for Private Practice Owners

In the last chapter, we discussed business planning. Your business plan is your blueprint that guides how you construct your business. Part of that plan is deciding on a business model. Your business model needs to support your mission—the actions that will lead you to your vision and help you fulfill your purpose.

If you're anything like me, your business model will change frequently as you build your legacy. But you may not anticipate exactly how those changes will take place. In 2018, when I handed my resignation in to the school district and decided to go full time in my private practice, I knew I eventually wanted to offer services to other business owners like the book you're reading now, but I didn't know exactly how that would shape up.

If you stay connected to your purpose and make decisions in alignment with your vision, the right opportunities for changing or expanding your business model will present themselves.

That's how it happened when I moved from a private practice to a group practice, and when I decided to offer coaching services for other business owners. I've adjusted my business model every time I've rewritten my business plan—over twenty at this point.

I never made those changes lightly; each and every time I adjusted my business model, it was the result of a SGOT analysis. I consciously look for opportunities for growth at regular intervals. When my private practice brought in over a million dollars in revenue, I knew it was time to share the systems and processes I used to build my business with other healthcare and mental health providers who wanted a massive impact and the sort of profit that would allow them to support their families and achieve their purpose in life.

We've discussed SGOT analysis in detail in previous chapters, so I won't go over it all again here, but if you need a refresher, turn to Chapter 6.

After you decide to modify your business model, you will need to share the plan with every stakeholder in your business. The people who work for you, your clients or customers, and anyone else who has a vested interest in the success of your business needs to know about changes, because it helps to renew their confidence in you and your business. Your stakeholders will appreciate that you are working to grow and improve because it further guarantees their position in the company.

After you let stakeholders know about your planned changes, you will need to create a step-by-step plan for implementation. I employ the assistance of a business coach for this step because sometimes, when you're in the thick of running your business, it can be difficult to see all the detailed work that needs to happen.

When I added business coaching services and opened a business-to-business section of SMPsychotherapy, I needed to consider the following:

What services I would offer, and to whom.

How I would offer those services.

What I needed to put in place to make those services possible.

How I would market those services.

For me, I needed to make sure I had a step-by-step plan for helping private practice owners set up a profitable, impactful business. That's when the Multi-Million-Dollar Private Practice Framework™ was born.

So, how do you decide on a business model?

First, you need to decide if you're offering services to consumers, other businesses, or both. Remember, this decision is not permanent. You can start offering consumer services now, and add business services later, like I did. You can also decide to stop offering a service at any time.

Once you understand your overall business model, you'll need to figure out how to deliver your services to those clients. Many of these ways of delivering services are useful with both business to consumer models, and business-to-business models.

MULTI-MILLION DOLLAR BUSINESS MODELS FOR PRIVATE PRACTICE OWNERS™

BUSINESS TO BUSINESS

BUSINESS TO CONSUMER

BUSINESS TO BUSINESS & BUSINESS TO CONSUMER

Method of Delivery:
★ Solo Sessions ★ Business ★ Coaching and Consulting
★ Subscription Based Services ★ Group Sessions ★ Retreats
★ Self-help Services ★ Website ★ Books ★ Online course

Methods of service delivery can include:

SOLO SESSIONS

In a business to consumer model private practice, solo sessions will likely make up much of what you offer. To ensure business success, plan exactly how you want your clients to feel in their sessions and after. How much time will you spend with them? What sort of follow-up will you offer? Will you accept insurance, be private pay, or run a hybrid model? Are your solo sessions offered via telehealth, in person, or a combination?

BUSINESS COACHING AND CONSULTING

As a business owner, you will have people ask to pick your brain about building a business on a regular basis. Don't fall into the trap of giving away your valuable knowledge for free. Instead, consider offering business-to-business services as a coach and consultant. You can help other people build their own successful private practice by showing them exactly how you built yours.

SUBSCRIPTION-BASED SERVICES

Subscription based services are a great way to keep clients loyal and offer greater value. For mental health professionals, a subscription that includes a certain number of sessions for six months or year can help ensure a client relationship that yields real results. Healthcare providers can consider a subscription to an online education portal for patients, or a subscription for certain concierge level services such as skin treatments.

GROUP SESSIONS

Offering group sessions for patients on everything from substance abuse to pain management or even healthy lifestyle choices can help your business serve more clients. Group sessions are led by you or another professional in your organization. These sessions increase both your profitability and your impact on the community.

If you decide to offer group sessions for a business-to-consumer model, you'll want to check on insurance regulations for group sessions and decide if these will be private pay or insurance pay.

If offering group coaching and consulting in a business-to-business model, consider what you have to offer other business owners, and what they will gain from working in collaboration with other private practice owners. Then, make a plan for the course, and start marketing!

RETREATS

You can host retreats for consumers or other businesses, so this option fits into both models. Perhaps you host a meditation and yoga retreat for clients and a business networking retreat for other CEOs. Get creative, brainstorm about what your ideal retreat looks like, and then hire an event planner who can make it a reality.

SELF-HELP SERVICES

Offering services clients can access on their own schedule is an incredible way to increase your impact on the world. By packaging courses, books, and other materials, you can help more people than your calendar allows you to meet with directly. What follows is a list of possible self-help services you can offer in either a business-to-consumer or a business-to-business model

YOUR WEBSITE

Your website is more than a marketing tool. It is an education hub that can help current and potential clients make decisions about their mental health from a place of education and compassion. That was my goal when I started my website. Today my email marketing efforts have an opening rate of about fifty percent, and I hear all the time from my practitioners that they use blog posts to guide sessions with clients or offer them as homework between sessions.

For my business-to-business website, I offer access to free information about running a private practice because I know not everyone can afford coaching. Make your resources valuable and useful and people will come to trust you. That makes them more likely to convert to paying customers in the future.

BOOKS

You have a specialty. Every therapist does. Take the area where you shine and write a book about it. Writing a book can draw in additional clients, serve as a resource to current clients, and position you as an expert in your field. That can lead to consulting work and public speaking opportunities.

Worried about your writing ability? Don't be. You have stories to tell and valuable insight to offer. Hire a team to help you do the rest. I'm not a native English speaker. In fact, one of my biggest insecurities has always been my writing ability. So, when I decided to write *Unbreakable* and to make my business website an educational hub, I hired support. I have a content writer, a writing coach, an editor, and a whole team of people helping to ensure my message is accessible. In every one of these situations, investing in support has yielded greater success than I dreamed possible.

ONLINE COURSES

Online courses can help you reach more people, which improves both your profitability and your impact on the world. Creating an online course requires some upfront investment of time and money but can pay you back in dividends. When you build an online course, you build a sustainable income stream that requires little day-to-day maintenance from you and your team. Online courses work for business-to-consumer and business-to-business services.

LICENSED PRODUCTS AND SERVICES

Do you have an online course that helps people create their own business, learn to use cognitive behavioral therapy effectively, or master rapport-building with clients? Turn that course into a licensed curriculum and market it to colleges and universities. The education sector is always looking for new, fresh ideas to improve their courses for future generations of mental health professionals.

Your business model is a part of your business plan that represents the services or products you want to offer the community you serve. Your model helps you make decisions about how to best serve those clients.

Are you feeling overwhelmed by the number of choices for how to deliver services? Take a deep breath. You do not have to do everything at once. In fact, I don't think you should. I think you should pick your business model and start with one or two modes of delivering services. Then, as your practice grows, and you complete SGOT analyses and client surveys, you'll uncover new opportunities for expansion. Refer back to this list every quarter to help you make those decisions.

My goal in this section is to encourage you to think bigger. Doing something new or changing your business's operations is scary because our brains are wired to keep the status quo. Your brain will tell you that you are doing too much and dreaming too big. You'll think that staying small is the right decision and that you don't need to expand. Your brain is comfortable doing this thing you're good at—this thing that is now without knowledge gaps. You've done the learning, and now your brain wants to settle in for twenty years of sameness. What's wrong with that? Well, if your purpose is to impact the world and connect people with your products or services because you solve a problem, then this question isn't about you and your comfort level. It's about helping more people.

Getting out of your comfort zone is required if you want to increase your reach. Your business model is not a fixed concept. It's merely a floor plan of your house. As your business changes, the business model you started with may require an addition or a repurposing of space just as your home would if your family grew.

CHAPTER TAKEAWAYS

- The right business model will guide your decisions about which products and services you reproduce and distribute to your clients.
- Your business model will likely change as your business grows.
- There are a variety of ways to achieve success in any business model, including one-on-one services, group offerings, speaking opportunities, books, and more.

Chapter 13

Multi-Million-Dollar Private Practice Business Structures

Words like "fear" and "panic" are not words you want to use when describing an experience, but that is precisely what I felt the first time I met with my new accountant. Yet, it led to one of the best decisions I have ever made. This is how I got on the right track to scale my business.

When SMPsychotherapy started, and my waitlist was longer than my to-do list, I quickly realized I needed to make some decisions about business finances and accounting. I also realized I needed more knowledge about both of those things.

So, I went accountant shopping. Someone from an online business owner group recommended Antonio Pascarella of Pascarella Accounting Group in Meriden, Connecticut.

We scheduled a face-to-face meeting at a coffee shop. Ninety minutes later, I understood business structures, but at least part of that ninety minutes was stressful. As we sat across from each other, caffeine cooling in front of us, Antonio detailed what he'd learned about my business from the documents I sent him.

"You are not paying yourself enough."

"But I have all these expenses for the business."

"If you don't pay yourself from your business, you will pay more in taxes."

Antonio went on to explain the differences between an LLC and an SCORP. I already had an LLC, but we discussed why moving to an SCORP was the right structure for my business. Antonio explained how paying myself a salary would lower my overall taxes and ensure I could continue to expand my business the way I wanted.

The more we talked, the more panic set in. How could I ensure I had enough to cover payroll, insurance, and other business expenses if I paid myself a salary? Would I be able to save for retirement? Fear took hold because this new milestone happened faster than I expected. That speed made me nervous. Getting out of your comfort zone is always terrifying. It felt like I was handing a level of control to Antonio. The fear I felt could have stopped me, but instead, it signaled me that I had an opportunity to learn and grow.

During that initial meeting, Antonio and I reviewed business structures, tax laws, and the implications for my business. I soon knew he was the right person for me to hire for three reasons. He came highly recommended, he had the services I needed, and because of the confidence he demonstrated during our meeting.

As Antonio explained what I needed to know, I could feel myself relax. The fear faded away as his confidence was mirrored in me. I was learning. I had found someone that would take the time to educate me and make sure I understood all the important points. Grasping this new knowledge gave me an assurance that I could make and would make the right decisions for my business. I had the right person to help me do that in Antonio.

Now that I had the education I needed, I decided to become an SCORP. Within hours, Antonio had my new SCORP all set up. I now understood what he was doing and why, so it was easy to give up control and allow him to help me with his expertise. He reviewed my books, discovered they needed to be corrected, and cleaned it all up. Thanks to Antonio, my books were well organized and accurate, and my business had the right structure to move forward, and most importantly, I was learning.

Over the next several months, I worked with Antonio to learn as much as possible about the different business structures to make informed decisions about SMPsychotherapy. With his guidance, we reviewed everything I needed to know about payroll, tax implications, and structure. I also learned how to make sure I paid myself a living wage. When I bought a house, I asked Antonio for documents. Everyone was amazed I had direct access to my accountant.

Your business structures are the load-bearing walls of your house and the support beams that ensure it is built to last. Including them in your business plan is a must to guide your decisions. Selecting the right business structure can ensure you meet all legal requirements and set your business up for the rate of growth you want. Choosing the right accountant makes all this happen.

I've been so happy with Antonio that I have become his biggest free advertiser. I've recommended him to all my employees and contractors, and I want you to benefit from his teaching too.

I asked Antonio to answer some questions for this book, so you can hear from him about some of the things you need to remember as a business owner.

Here are a few things I asked:

Antonio, why is it so important to hire the right accountant?

Bottom line: It is for the business owner's peace of mind. Knowing the IRS is not going to come back to you, having messy books, etc. You won't have to pay to fix mistakes.

What about those who want to save money by keeping their own books or finding a cheap accountant?

Don't try to be a bookkeeper on your own. This may save you money short term, but it may cause you more significant problems down the road. It makes no sense to save a few hundred dollars instead of focusing on marketing efforts that could make thousands.

During tax season, people look for a tax accountant that charges less than others.

People call to ask how much I charge per hour. I am not the least expensive accountant, but I don't work for a client for forty hours a week. I work about four hours a month for average clients. That monthly expense isn't much money considering what you get out of it.

The cheaper you get, the worse service you get, and that means mistakes are made.

Tell me about one of the mistakes you've seen.

I worked with an owner who had a CPA. This CPA used their own interpretation of the accounting standards. Seven years of transactions were misclassified. Some things were not classified at all. This took me months to undo. There were tax implications, penalties, and amended returns for the previous three years. It ended up being a 30,000 to 40,000 dollar mistake.

Forty thousand dollars? That makes me gasp. That's why I wanted to be educated. I hired you because you took the time to educate me. Ignorance has huge consequences.

Exactly.

And you said a CPA did this?

Having a CPA doesn't mean anything. The difference between a CPA and a non-CPA is that a CPA can do public audits of companies. Everyone has to follow the same accounting standards.

What's another mistake people make?

Not thinking about taxes before the end of the year. You have all transactions posted, but the owner doesn't do anything to look at financials before the end of the year to plan for taxes. Then you are only working with after-the-fact numbers, and there is nothing you can do,

I look at the books before the end of the year and determine how we can move forward. We need to know what is going to happen and whether it's a positive or negative outcome.

By doing the review before the end of the year, we can determine if a large expense can offset some revenue to reduce tax implications. We can look at the bottom line and see if we like it or if we need to lower it.

What should a business owner look for when hiring an accountant?

You have to trust the person you hire to guide you through the tax implications of your business. Many accountants will give you the answers you want.

Pay attention to how the CPA or accountant educates you. Are they giving you all the information you need to know to make good decisions for your business? Look at how invested the accountant is in helping you understand.

Let's expand on that. What are some traits or characteristics we should look for in an accountant?

There are a few important qualities. Personalized attention is a must. That requires availability. You want someone who you can reach when you have questions or need something addressed. Knowledge, certainly. Someone who can educate you and that takes having a thorough grasp of the information enough to teach it. It also means taking the time to educate the client. Then you need accuracy and transparency. A client should insist on all of these traits in their accountant.

What do you recommend business owners do to prepare for taxes?

Save thirty percent for federal taxes and five percent for state. Make quarterly payments, so you don't have a huge bill at the end of the year. Some people wait until the end of the year, and that can mean a huge tax bill and penalties and interest.

Is it important for business owners to have the same accountant for their personal taxes and their business for consistency?

Consistency can be important. Changing your accountant every year is the worst thing you can do because things can get lost. Some accountants don't even ask for last year's tax returns. They won't know if you're carrying a loss over from one year to the next. You want support for everything that could happen throughout the year. H&R Block and others close their offices on April 15th. You want someone you can call in July.

This year, I have a new client who always did her taxes with TurboTax. She wanted to call me during the year, and I can do that for her. It's a five or ten-minute conversation, and there's no charge.

An accountant has to know the client, not just the business. I have to know what they want to accomplish and when they want to accomplish it.

Then we look at the business and what the business can do for you. You should reach your personal goals, and you can't do that unless you reach the business goals.

Antonio is so right. You can only reach your personal goals if you reach your business goal. That is why it is vital to understand your goals, plan for your future, and have the right people in place to help you reach that dream. Antonio Pascarella has been the right accountant for me, and you will need to find the right one for you.

As you search for your accountant, I want to give you all the knowledge necessary to avoid the fear and apprehension that I had to experience in my initial meeting. Thanks to Antonio, I now understand and can share with you the basics of business structure. Of course, there is a disclaimer. The questions that Antonio answered and the information I'll share in the rest of this chapter are no substitute for direct legal advice and accounting assistance, so know that this is for educational purposes to assist you as you seek the proper help and have those crucial conversations.

THE TYPES OF BUSINESS STRUCTURES

- Sole Proprietorship: A sole proprietorship is a business structure where an individual owns and operates a business as a single person. You can operate a sole proprietorship as an LLC or as an informal business structure.
- Limited Liability Company (LLC): A Limited Liability Company (LLC) is a popular business structure that provides liability protection with some tax benefits. An LLC can be an SCORP, C-corp, or Sole Proprietorship.
- S corporation (SCORP): An S corporation (SCORP) is a type of business structure that provides the benefits of a corporation. An LLC can also be an SCORP.
- C corporation (C-corp): A C corporation (C-Corp) is a type of business structure that is a separate legal entity from its owners. An LLC can also operate as a C-corp

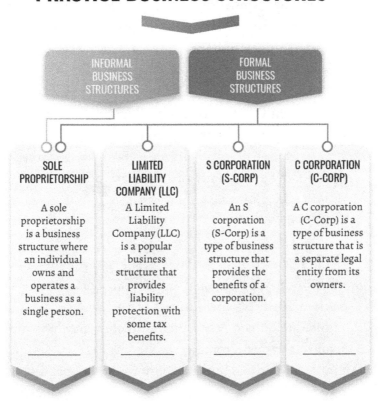

MULTI-MILLION DOLLAR PRIVATE PRACTICE BUSINESS STRUCTURES™

INFORMAL BUSINESS STRUCTURES

FORMAL BUSINESS STRUCTURES

SOLE PROPRIETORSHIP

A sole proprietorship is a business structure where an individual owns and operates a business as a single person.

LIMITED LIABILITY COMPANY (LLC)

A Limited Liability Company (LLC) is a popular business structure that provides liability protection with some tax benefits.

S CORPORATION (S-CORP)

An S corporation (S-Corp) is a type of business structure that provides the benefits of a corporation.

C CORPORATION (C-CORP)

A C corporation (C-Corp) is a type of business structure that is a separate legal entity from its owners.

THE PROS AND CONS OF A SOLE PROPRIETORSHIP

A sole proprietorship is common for startup businesses. It is a good choice when looking for a simple and easy-to-manage business structure.

PROS:

1. Easy to start: Starting a sole proprietorship is relatively easy and inexpensive compared to some other structures.
2. Complete control: The sole proprietor has full control over the business and can make all decisions.
3. Simple tax structure: A sole proprietorship has a simple tax structure. All profits and losses from the business are reported on the owner's personal income tax return, and the owner pays taxes on the profits.
4. Low operational costs: Since the business is owned and operated by a single person, there are no additional costs associated with hiring employees.

CONS:

1. Unlimited personal liability: A sole proprietorship does not protect your personal assets. Your personal assets can be used to pay off any business debts.
2. Limited resources: A sole proprietorship may have limited resources to operate and grow the business.
3. Limited lifespan: A sole proprietorship depends on the owner. If the owner dies or becomes incapacitated, the business may be dissolved.
4. Difficulty in raising capital: Since a sole proprietorship is a one-person operation, raising capital through lenders and investors can be challenging.

THE PROS AND CONS OF LIMITED LIABILITY COMPANIES (LLCS)

A Limited Liability Company (LLC) can provide significant benefits, particularly in liability protection. However, it is more complex.

Be aware that certain healthcare professionals may need to establish a Professional Limited Liability Company (PLLC). A PLLC is a specialized type of LLC designed for professionals that provides limited liability protection while allowing them to operate their businesses as licensed professionals.

If you have a partner in your private practice, you may consider setting up a Limited Liability Partnership. (LLP), combining a partnership's features with the LLC's limited liability protection.

PROS:

1. Limited liability: LLC owners are not personally responsible for the company's debts and liabilities. To have this liability protection, you must separate business and personal checking accounts, credit cards, etc.

2. Flexible tax structure: An LLC is taxed as an individual with self-employment taxes, which means that profits and losses appear on the owner's personal tax returns, avoiding double taxation. Your structure affects your tax rate, which can affect your personal income, retirement, and other financial aspects of your business.

3. Easy to set up and maintain: Setting up and maintaining an LLC is relatively easy compared to a corporation to an SCORP or C-Corp.

CONS:

1. Cost of set up: Setting up an LLC can be more expensive than a sole proprietorship due to the need for formal documents and state registration.

2. Self-employment taxes: LLC members are subject to self-employment taxes, which can be higher than the taxes paid by employees of a corporation.

3. Limited lifespan: Like a sole proprietorship, an LLC is dependent on the owners, and if the owners die or leave the company, the LLC may be dissolved.

4. Complexity in decision-making: Once you move past a sole proprietorship, other people may be involved in the company, creating a more complex management structure.

THE PROS AND CONS OF AN S CORPORATION (SCORP)

When your business grows to a revenue of $50,000 per year, you have the option of starting an S corporation (SCORP). Still, a higher rate of revenue is usually desired. This is done for tax purposes, since an SCORP can help avoid huge tax bills.

With an SCORP, you put yourself on the payroll, avoiding self-employment taxes. An SCORP can also set company matching policies for social security taxes and retirement planning.

PROS:

1. Limited liability: Like a traditional corporation, S corporations offer personal liability protection.

2. Tax benefits: S corporations can pass through profits and losses to shareholders' personal tax returns, avoiding double taxation. An SCORP is not subject to federal income tax.

3. Easy to raise capital: S corporations can raise capital by selling stock to investors, which can help the business grow and expand.

CONS:

1. Formalities: S corporations must follow strict formalities, such as keeping detailed records of business decisions.

2. Cost of set-up: Setting up an S corporation can be more expensive than other business structures due to the need for formal documents and state registration.

3. Limited flexibility in allocations: S corporations are subject to strict rules governing the allocation of profits and losses.

THE PROS AND CONS OF A C-CORP

A C-Corporation can be a beneficial business structure for businesses requiring liability protection and planning long-term growth and expansion.

PROS:

1. Limited liability: C-Corps offer personal liability protection.

2. Separate legal entity: C-Corps are a separate legal entity from their owners, allowing the corporation to own property, enter into contracts, and sue or be sued in its own name.

3. Continued existence: C-Corps can continue to exist even after the death of their owners, ensuring that the business can continue to operate and grow.

CONS:

1. Double taxation: C-Corps are subject to double taxation, meaning that profits are taxed at the corporate level and then again when distributed as dividends to shareholders.

2. Formalities: C-Corps must follow strict formalities, such as holding annual shareholder meetings and keeping detailed records of business decisions.

3. Cost of set-up: Setting up a C-Corp can be more expensive than other business structures due to the need for formal documents and state registration.

4. Complex management structure: C-Corps are a larger business entity creating a more complex management structure.

I began my journey into expanding my business with fear, apprehension, and nerves, but I don't make decisions based on fear. Solid business decisions are made with knowledge and information, and that requires education. Antonio Pascarella took the time to educate me, and as I learned, my fear subsided and my confidence grew.

With education and confidence, I was able to make the structural decisions that have allowed my business to flourish. I want the same for you. Find the right accountant, get educated, and make the business structure decisions that will support your dreams.

CHAPTER TAKEAWAYS

- Choosing the right legal structure or your business can help you make decisions about taxes, profit, and hiring.
- You can keep things informal with a sole-proprietorship or make a normal business structure by establishing an LLC.
- An LLC can be a sole-proprietorship, an SCORP or a C-CORP.
- Hiring an accountant who is willing to educate you about your options is the best path toward success.

Chapter 14

Multi-Million-Dollar Marketing Plan Framework™

Marketing is more than just a buzzword or a set of tactics. It is a fundamental part of how your business connects with clients, builds relationships, and ultimately thrives. As a business owner, I understand the emotional investment that goes into every marketing campaign. It can be both a daunting task and one of the most rewarding aspects of running a business.

Effective marketing is more important than ever in today's fast-paced digital world. It's not enough to simply offer a great product or service. You need to tell the world about it in a way that resonates with your target audience. This requires a deep understanding of your customers' needs and desires, as well as a willingness to engage in a variety of marketing strategies.

I've learned that marketing is not just about promoting a product or service; it's about creating a connection with your clients that goes beyond the transaction. It's about building a brand that people trust and believe in, and that takes time, dedication, and a willingness to put yourself out there.

In this chapter, I want to share my insights and experiences with marketing and offer practical advice that can help you create effective campaigns that deliver results. A million-dollar marketing plan is how to take your business to an elite level.

OVERCOMING HESITATION AND FEAR

Marketing can be a complex topic because of the emotional response some people experience. You may be uncomfortable marketing yourself, feeling like it is selfish or manipulative as you try to convince people to buy your services over other local businesses.

You may feel awkward about the competitive nature of marketing as you seek to persuade potential clients that you are their best option. Let's explore a few of these potential hesitations.

- Fear of failure: One of the biggest reasons for emotional hesitation in marketing is the fear of failure. Many worry that their marketing efforts will not be successful and that others will judge or criticize them. This fear can be especially strong for new business owners or those who have had negative experiences with marketing.

- Lack of confidence: Another reason for emotional hesitation in marketing is a lack of confidence in your abilities. This can be due to a lack of experience or knowledge about marketing, or it can be a more general lack of self-confidence that affects all aspects of your business.

- Concerns about authenticity: Some people may worry that marketing their business will make them appear inauthentic or "salesy." They may be concerned that aggressively promoting their services will turn people off and damage their reputation.

- Personal insecurities: Emotional hesitation in marketing can also stem from personal insecurities and discomfort with a "look at me" endeavor. For example, someone may feel uncomfortable promoting themselves due to their introverted nature.

- Ethical concerns: Finally, some people may be emotionally hesitant to market themselves and their businesses because of ethical concerns. They may worry that marketing tactics are manipulative and that the product or service should stand on its own merit.

If any of this describes you, here are some practices that can help you overcome your hesitation:

Get in touch with those feelings. Determine why you feel that way. Have you had bad experiences? Has someone convinced you that marketing is wrong or distasteful? Once you understand where those feelings originate, you can address them based on additional evidence.

Remember your mission. You started your business to help people. The simple fact is you cannot help if they don't know you exist. People are out there who need your help. Your services could change their lives. Don't let your feelings rob them of the knowledge that helping is your mission.

Think of how many people you could help. Not only do you want to help people, but you want to help as many as possible. This is the reason to embrace all forms of marketing. Helping as many people as possible means reaching as many as possible through your marketing strategy.

QUESTIONS TO GET STARTED

There are a variety of methods to market your business. All will be beneficial, but depending on your goals, you may emphasize some methods over others. Marketing strategies need to change as your business changes. Regular evaluation of your goals and marketing strategy is crucial as you move from starting a private practice to growing your business and expanding your services. Consider the following questions as you evaluate your marketing plan:

- Who do you want to target? (Think about age group, gender, profession, life stage, etc.)
- What do you want your hourly rate/pricing to be?
- Where will you offer your services or sell products? Will you have a location or work online only?
- What is the potential market for your business in your area?
- What existing services and products are already in the area you plan to cover?
- Is the marketplace crowded?
- What skills and professional credentials do you have or can you develop to help you stand out?

THE VALUE OF CREATING A STRONG BRAND

Developing a strong brand is the heart and soul of marketing. It can help differentiate your business from competitors, build trust and credibility with clients, and create long-lasting relationships. It's not just about selling a product or service, but about creating an emotional connection with clients. It's what makes your business memorable, relatable, and trustworthy.

It all starts with understanding your business's mission and purpose. Ask yourself, what is the driving force behind your business? What values do you hold dear? What kind of personality do you want your brand to embody? These questions help you develop a brand identity that aligns with your business's core values and speaks to your target audience.

Throughout this book, I've stated that your business is a reflection of you. That is true of your branding as well. You are your brand, and your brand is you. Make sure the values and traits that characterize your brand are ones you embody.

Once you've established your brand identity, the next step is to bring it to life through visual elements such as a logo, tagline, and color scheme. These elements should reflect your brand's personality and values and be consistent across all your marketing strategies. Cohesive branding creates a powerful visual identity that builds recognition and helps your business stand out in a crowded marketplace.

However, creating a strong brand is more than just design and messaging. It's about creating an exceptional customer experience that builds loyalty and trust. Every interaction a client has with your brand should be positive and seamless from the first moment of awareness. By creating a client-focused experience, you establish yourself as a reliable and trustworthy brand.

It's also crucial to continually evolve your brand strategy. That means keeping an eye on customer needs and desires, adapting to changing market trends, and refining your brand messaging and visual identity. By staying in tune with your audience, you can create a brand that resonates deeply and inspires loyalty for years to come.

COMPONENTS OF YOUR MARKETING PLAN

Your marketing plan is your roadmap, outlining the specific activities that will be used to reach the target audience and achieve the desired outcomes. A well-crafted marketing plan considers a range of factors and creates a cohesive and effective strategy. In this section, we will explore the key components of a marketing plan and the role they play in driving the success of a marketing campaign.

- Begin with a SGOT analysis. You cannot engage in effective marketing unless you know who you are and what you do. As you analyze your strengths, growth areas, opportunities, and threats, you will see what your potential clients need to know to connect with you and your company.

- Define your target audience: Before you begin any marketing campaign, it is crucial to identify your target audience. Who are you trying to reach? What are their needs, desires, issues, and problems? By defining your target audience, you can tailor your marketing efforts to resonate with their specific interests and concerns. Detail your ideal client's demographics, such as age, income level, and location, as well as psychographics, such as the problems your company can solve and the worries and fears they have.

- Set clear goals: It is important to establish clear goals for your marketing efforts. By setting specific, measurable goals, you can track your progress and adjust your marketing strategy accordingly. Your goals should contain specific actions as well as a revenue goal.

- Develop a plan: Your plan should include a clear message, a defined target audience, a budget, and a timeline for implementation. With a plan in place, you can take action and begin executing your marketing efforts.

- Experiment with different opportunities: a wide variety of marketing opportunities exist, including social media, email marketing, content marketing, and paid advertising. I will discuss these in detail as we move through this chapter. It is important to experiment with different opportunities to determine which ones are most effective for your business. In my professional life, I have been able to expand beyond these into radio and television opportunities. I'm open to every opportunity, as every business owner should be.

- Monitor and adjust: Once you begin implementing your marketing plan, it is important to monitor your results and make adjustments as needed. Use analytics tools to track your progress and identify areas for improvement. By continuously monitoring and adjusting your marketing efforts, you can stay on track and achieve your goals.

MULTI-MILLION DOLLAR MARKETING PLAN FRAMEWORK™

TRADITIONAL MARKETING

* Direct Mail Marketing
* Conferences and Network Events
* Local Business Partnerships
* Introduction Letters and Brochures
* Spend time where your ideal clients are

&

ONLINE MARKETING

* Social Media
* Website
* SEO
* Email Marketing
* Online Conferences and Network Events

EFFECTIVE TRADITIONAL OFFLINE MARKETING STRATEGY

In a world of digital media, some may assume that traditional marketing efforts are outdated and a waste of time and money. This is not the case. Traditional offline marketing can be an effective element of your strategy.

This could include:

* Print advertisements
* Direct mail marketing
* Connecting with area businesses and looking for partnership opportunities

- Sending introduction letters and brochures to related businesses
- Researching where your ideal clients are and spend time there
- Finding conferences and network events for your niche and attend. Hand out business cards and brochures to make connections

Marketing is about making a connection. The more opportunities you have to connect with new clients, potential clients, and referral sources, the faster you will meet your goals and create the massive impact you desire.

AN ENGAGING SOCIAL MEDIA AND ONLINE PRESENCE

Consider digital marketing as your virtual front office and waiting room. It is where people will form first impressions, gain information about your services, assess the quality of your business, and develop a comfort level with you and other clinicians and professionals on your staff.

As you develop your online marketing strategy, make sure you follow these fundamental principles:

DEVELOP A PROFESSIONAL WEBSITE DESIGN

Secure your own domain name related to your business and then develop a great website. If you do not possess the ability of web design at a high level, hire a professional.

PROVIDE ONLINE EDUCATION

Marketing is more than an exclusive focus on sales. Free online educational services can assist your mission of helping people and demonstrate precisely the kind of help you can provide. Education demonstrates to the customer how they can benefit from your services.

These can include:

- Blogs
- Website Specialty Pages
- Podcast
- Webinars

When I provide free education, I am not just giving things away for free. It is an investment. When I take the opportunity to provide education, I am setting myself up as the expert. It allows me to show how I am different from everyone else.

Anybody with a license can do therapy. I want my clients to know exactly why I am the right therapist for them, and why my practice is the right choice for their entire family. Providing education builds trust, shows I am the go-to person, and allows clients to feel as if they know me and my practice before they even come to their first appointment.

Education helps put the client at ease and allows them to feel the following:

- Educated
- Empowered
- Cared for
- Important
- Confident in decision-making
- Clear about the therapeutic process

UTILIZE SEARCH-ENGINE OPTIMIZATION (SEO)

When writing web pages and blogs, it is crucial to utilize SEO. This is the use of specific words and phrases so that search engines notice your blog, article, or webpage. There's also a technical side of SEO that you must consider during the initial set-up of your website. This helps potential clients find your online marketing rather than have it lost in the sea of internet information. To use SEO, it's best to hire a professional content writing service and web designer so that you are free to work in your area of genius rather than spend your time learning and fumbling through a DIY project.

DEVELOP A SOCIAL MEDIA PRESENCE

Facebook ads, Instagram ads, LinkedIn, and other social media can help spread your message, provide educational tips, and direct clients to resources. You can leverage paid ads with regular posts across social media platforms to get the best results. I also recommend hiring a social media marketing specialist if you aren't adept at posting and content creation.

DEVELOP AN EMAIL MARKETING CAMPAIGN

Email marketing campaigns can be a cost-effective and efficient way to connect through newsletters or educational materials. Much like a mail campaign using traditional mail, email campaigns need to be well presented, target the right people, and informative. When designing your email campaign, follow these general guidelines:

- Define your target audience
- Build your email list (many people give something away for free in exchange for collecting email addresses)
- Create your email content
- Design your email template
- Set up your email automation
- Measure your results

Social media, email campaigns, and online marketing allow clients to learn about your areas of expertise and the services you provide and grow comfortable with you and your company before ever stepping into your office. Take advantage of this powerful resource to grow your business.

STAY IN CONTACT WITH OTHER PROFESSIONALS

Staying in touch with other professionals is an important way to network and inform others of your work. Professional referrals are an important aspect of building your practice. Accomplishing this requires that you market yourself to other businesses.

Business-to-business marketing for therapists and healthcare professionals can be a highly effective way to reach potential clients and build a strong referral network. Here are some strategies that you can use:

ESTABLISH RELATIONSHIPS

As a therapist or healthcare provider, you likely work with other professionals, such as physicians, psychiatrists, social workers, and other therapists. Building strong relationships with these professionals can be a valuable source of referrals.

Also, consider reaching out to other professionals, such as attorneys, to introduce yourself and your services. Offer to meet with them in person or provide them with information about your practice, such as brochures or business cards. I built relationships with several attorneys and launched a service for immigration evaluations for people dealing with deportation and other immigration struggles.

ATTEND INDUSTRY EVENTS AND CONFERENCES

Attending industry events and conferences can be an effective way to connect with other professionals and stay up-to-date on the latest trends and research in your field. Look for events and conferences that are relevant to your practice and attend with the goal of networking and making connections.

OFFER TRAINING AND EDUCATION

As I discussed previously, education sets you up as an expert. This is not limited to the view of clients. It can also apply to other professionals. Offering training and education sessions for other professionals in your field can be a great way to establish yourself as an expert in your area of practice and build relationships with other professionals. You could offer in-person training sessions and webinars or even create educational content that can be shared on your website or social media channels.

Writing books in your area of expertise is also a valuable way to provide educational content. Often, these books aren't huge revenue generators by themselves—royalties don't add up to much—but using them to connect with a wider audience, launch a speaking career, or establish yourself as an expert can go a long way in ensuring the long-term health of your business.

COLLABORATE WITH OTHER BUSINESSES

Look for opportunities to collaborate with other businesses in your area. For example, you could partner with a wellness center to offer therapy services to their clients. Collaborating with other businesses can be a great way to expand your reach and build your referral network.

LEVERAGING PROFESSIONAL SERVICES FOR CONTENT CREATION AND BRANDING

Hiring professional services has already been mentioned, but it is worth exploring in more detail. As a healthcare or mental health professional, you need to spend much of your time providing services to your clients. As a business owner, you are called upon to perform many duties, and working in your area of genius is the best way to ensure success. Leveraging professional service can be the solution you need to have stunning content and branding while you focus on serving clients. You can receive valuable assistance through the following:

- Professional writing services
- Content creation services
- Online copywriting services
- Branding services

Leveraging professional services in marketing is crucial to achieving success in today's competitive business environment. Professional services can help you reach your target audience, build your brand, and stand out in a crowded marketplace.

I have benefited from a writing coach, public speaking coach, content writing company, web designer, social media strategist, and branding consultant. Sure, it looks like I'm always writing, posting, and running webinars, but the reality is I built a team to help with marketing so I can narrow my focus to where I can have the most impact.

Each person I've hired to support marketing efforts has helped me develop my expertise and grow my business. By leveraging the expertise of professionals in marketing, you can achieve your business goals and thrive in your mission.

Successful marketing is all about connecting with people, building relationships, and educating the public while growing your business. It's a journey that requires dedication, effort, strategy, and a willingness to push through any hesitation or doubts. By focusing on your clients and your abilities, getting the help you need, and putting in the effort, you can create marketing strategies that drive results. Furthermore, it will inspire and empower along the way. Remember, marketing is not selfish; it's the best way to help your future clients find you and create the massive impact you hope to have on the world.

To help you on your marketing journey, I'd like to offer you The Multi-Million-Dollar Marketing Plan Assessment. Marketing is the most difficult part of business for many people I work with. This assessment will help you figure out what's stopping you from marketing your practice effectively and give you detailed feedback on the best marketing strategies to help you build a profitable, impactful business.

BOOK YOUR MARKETING ASSESSMENT

CHAPTER TAKEAWAYS

- Feeling hesitant about marketing is common, but you must work to overcome any fear because marketing is how you fulfill your purpose.
- Marketing efforts must keep your ideal client in mind.
- A strong brand is crucial for marketing success.

- An SGOT analysis will help you craft a successful marketing plan.
- Including a wide variety of methods in your marketing plan will help you reach more people.
- Traditional marketing strategies such as direct mail, print ads, and networking events are valuable.
- Effective digital marketing will require you to hire support so you can focus your energy in your area of genius.
- Giving knowledge and resources away for free (like a blog or downloadable guide) can help build trust with prospective clients.

Chapter 15

Multi-Million-Dollar Private Practice Hiring Framework™

You are now a business owner, or soon will be. Your past has prepared you for this. You have had enough success to give you the confidence to own your own business. There may have been times you were frustrated working with people who didn't have your drive, work ethic, or ability. Now your business is your dream, livelihood, and future. All of this leads to a set of beliefs and practices which may include:

- No one will care for your business like you
- You have to do everything alone
- You have trouble trusting others
- You only feel confident having your business in your own hands

Your confidence and work ethic are admirable, but carrying the entire load of your business yourself is a poor strategy and is doomed to fail.

No one has every gift. No matter how talented you are, you are not a jack of all trades. Even if you can carry out multiple tasks, there is not enough time to do everything your business needs. Then, there is your own well-being to consider. Carrying too much for too long leads to burnout, physical health issues, mental fatigue, a loss of connection with your purpose, and problems in relationships. Your business needs you at your best, and that will mean you need a qualified team around you.

It is time to evaluate your personal story that has led to your beliefs that tell you that you must do everything yourself and put the needs of your business above your own. To build your thriving business, you will need top talent thriving in their areas of competency with strong employee retention. Of course, your hiring process will be open to people of any ethnicity with equal employment opportunity practices. This will require guarding against unconscious bias and instituting hiring practices that attract the best candidates. You want to hire qualified people who believe in and support the vision and mission of your company.

In this chapter, I will show you those hiring practices. I'll discuss who to hire and when and give you my Seven Step Hiring for Success Framework. This will empower you to engage the best people for your business and get them properly onboarded.

However, no business owner is perfect, and knowing this leads to the fear of hiring the wrong person. It's true. There may be occasions when you hire someone that does not align with your business and must be let go. This can be uncomfortable, but it is not a personal reflection on you. It is a necessary part of business. It should not hinder you from building your team and growing your business. I will show you how to address the situation when an employee must be let go.

That's a lot of important ground to cover, so let's begin with when to make your first hires.

DETERMINING WHO TO HIRE AND WHEN TO HIRE THEM

The answer to when to hire people is straightforward. The answer is: immediately. You need to hire people when you decide to start a business. From the beginning, adjust your mindset to put aside any struggles accepting help, feelings of discomfort asking for support, or control issues. Your mindset needs to work toward building a team that can support your business goals.

You need to be working in your area of genius and putting others in a place to do the same. When others are thriving in their area of genius, your business is multiplying genius with every employee. You are able to trust in their skill and empower them to grow. This leads to happy employees, high retention, and trusted competency throughout your business. This is how businesses thrive.

Next, let me answer the question of who to hire. Your first hire needs to be a coach.

When I started my business, I did not have significant resources. Yet, I knew in order to run a successful business, I needed someone that could coach me on exactly how to do it in my situation. It was not easy to pay for the right coach, but learning by trial and error is a lot more expensive. Early in my business, all the money I made went right back into supporting and growing my skill set as a business owner. Find someone who has done what you want to do and hire them as your coach.

Remember, this is not a hobby. This is your business. Treat it as a business from the outset and hire the expert help you need for it to thrive. If you simply want a hobby, it is fine to dabble and just see what works. Hobbies allow you the luxury of learning as you go, and trial and error is a legitimate method. Business is different. You can't afford to guess. It is a waste of time, energy, and money. Get your coach in place immediately to set your business on the right track.

You need to hire two other positions from the outset as well: a mentor and a consultant. Each one plays a unique role in your success.

BUSINESS COACH

A business coach works with business owners, executives, and entrepreneurs to help them develop skills, overcome obstacles, and achieve their goals. A business coach may not have the exact type of business you want to grow, but they understand how business and leadership work. They focus on enhancing the individual's performance, often in areas such as leadership, management, communication, and personal development. A business coach typically provides guidance, support, and accountability to help their clients reach their full potential. A business coach will not tell you what to do, but will guide you in making the best decisions.

BUSINESS MENTOR

A business mentor is a more experienced person who provides guidance, advice, and support to less experienced individuals. The right mentor will have done exactly what you aim to achieve. They share their knowledge, experience, and skills to help their mentees navigate the business world and make informed decisions. A business mentor helps their mentee to develop new skills, gain confidence, and achieve their goals. Sometimes you may find a mentor organically who is willing to support you without charging for their time. Most of the time, however, you will get more individualized attention and support if you financially compensate a mentor.

BUSINESS CONSULTANT

While a coach is a guide, and a mentor is a been-there-done-that support, a consultant is an expert who will tell you exactly how to get where you want to be. A business consultant provides expert advice and solutions to businesses to help them overcome specific challenges or achieve specific goals. They use their expertise in a particular area, such as finance, marketing, or operations, to analyze a business's operations, identify areas for improvement, and provide recommendations for changes or strategies. A business consultant may also help businesses implement new processes, technology, or management practices to improve their performance.

This is your brain trust. It is the team that helps you grow personally and professionally to thrive in business and be your best self in the process. They provide you with a wealth of experience and can share their own painful lessons so you don't have to experience those yourself. You are not an expert at everything, and that is fine. Hire people who are experts and use their knowledge and guidance. This is the fastest and most efficient way to build the business of your dreams.

In a perfect world, you can find someone who is a coach that provides guidance, a mentor who has done what you want to do, and a consultant who is an expert at running a thriving business. If you find that person, pay them what they're worth and hold on tight. Your business will thrive.

SUPPORT STAFF

Once you have the proper coaching and guidance, you need to delegate the things that take you away from your area of genius and time working with clients. Your next round of hires needs to include the following areas:

- Billing
- Credentialing
- Accountant and taxes
- Administration and office work, e.g., phone calls and scheduling

Having this team of coaching and support staff in place gives you what you need to build your private practice. You will have the collective knowledge of your experience, plus your coach, mentor, and consultant, giving you the wisdom and insight to build that strong, thriving business. Then, with the help of your support staff, you will have the time and energy to focus on clients and growing your business.

HIRING INDEPENDENT CONTRACTORS, W-2 EMPLOYEES, OR BOTH

Many private practice owners start out thinking they will be solo practitioners. This will change once your waitlist begins expanding. There may also be needs for bilingual practitioners or those with additional skills beyond your own. This is when you will need to start formulating job postings.

There are two important considerations here. First is the laws of your state. The state laws vary regarding 1099 contractors, so be sure you are following the laws of your state. The second consideration is your business model. It will determine your recruitment strategies for job candidates.

In my private practice, I prefer hiring independent contractors. There are several reasons for this. I want therapists to feel a sense of independence. I want them to earn more money and feel in control of their own career. Of course, there are rules, guidelines, and expectations, but therapists in my private practice have the freedom to do their work their own way. This is in regard to scheduling and other such matters. They are in charge of their own daily practice.

I also use independent contractors in office positions, such as scheduling and payroll. However, there are exceptions. Some of my administrative staff are W-2 employees.

So check the laws in your state and then hire based on your business model.

MULTI-MILLION-DOLLAR PRIVATE PRACTICE HIRING FRAMEWORK™

1. TAKE CONTROL OF THE APPLICATION PROCESS

2. SCHEDULE INITIAL PHONE INTERVIEWS

3. SCHEDULE ZOOM INTERVIEWS

4. FINAL INTERVIEW

5. MAKE THE HIRE

6. ONBOARDING AND TRAINING

7. CHECK-INS WITH STAFF

Hiring can seem daunting if you have never done it before, but you do not have to feel anxious. Follow my Seven-Step Hiring for Success Framework, and you will have the process you need to build your team.

STEP 1: TAKE CONTROL OF THE APPLICATION PROCESS

Write a great job posting and find the best places to post it. There is no one method of finding potential candidates. Internet platforms for job seekers, such as Indeed, can be effective. Social media can be used in recruiting, and don't dismiss word of mouth.

In my experience, Indeed has been the best posting site for the investment I make. Ninety percent of my therapists come from Indeed. Five percent come from word of mouth. The final five percent are people who have seen my work, believed in my vision, and sought me out, wanting to be part of this movement.

This is a demonstration of how important marketing is to your business. It not only draws clients, but it may inspire professionals to want to join you in your mission because they believe in your vision,

I personally go through all applications. This may be a team process in the future, but for now, I want to look at each candidate myself. This hands-on approach makes me highly knowledgeable about the people I eventually hire. I can then do a great job matching therapists to clients. I only assign clients based on the ideal client of that therapist in their specialty.

To get to know your candidates, several tools and practices can be helpful. Some of these include:

- Using personality tests
- Conducting background checks
- Confirming resume information and candidate experience. This is true for part-time, full-time, independent contractors, or employees. Not everyone is honest on their resume
- Providing potential candidates with a questionnaire to screen candidates

STEP 2: SCHEDULE INITIAL PHONE INTERVIEWS

The first interview is a thirty-minute phone call. I provide them with questions before the call to see how they fit my business needs. Questions include:

- Are they looking for full-time or part-time?
- Are they fully licensed?
- What is their availability?
- Discuss aspects of their resume

STEP 3: SCHEDULE ZOOM INTERVIEWS

For those candidates that match up well with the job opening, schedule a second interview via Zoom. This is where we talk about items such as:

- Mission
- Vision
- Ideal clients
- The candidates' future aspirations and goals

STEP 4: FINAL INTERVIEW

When candidates seem to be a good fit, I do a final interview where we talk about items such as:

- Their interest in working for my company
- Their alignment with the vision and mission
- Details of their theoretical approach

At this point, however, it is more than tangible items. It is about their energy. Do they bring the intangible elements that will fit nicely into my business? The process involves lots of information gathering and evaluation. Still, there is also a measure of following your gut and trusting your instincts.

STEP 5: MAKE THE HIRE

Once I have decided to hire, I send them an offer. Employees receive an offer letter. Independent contractors receive a contract. Then, they are connected with HR.

STEP 6: ONBOARDING AND TRAINING

It is essential that your new hires are clear on the expectations of their job description, understand your company culture, and fit well into their new work environment. This requires an effective onboarding process. Approach the onboarding of employees and contractors as equal to onboarding clients.

This is a two-step process:

- Get connected as a team member. Getting a new hire onboarding as a team member includes items such as:
  - » writing a profile
  - » professional photo for the website
  - » human resources paperwork
  - » credentialing
  - » billing
- Training. In the training process, make sure the following items are covered and emphasized:
  - » Job expectations and responsibilities
  - » Provide a copy of the procedure manual
  - » Provide calendar dates
  - » Develop a marketing plan for each practitioner that promotes their specific skills.

STEP 7: CHECK-INS WITH STAFF

Once the hire is made, it may be tempting to return to your daily work, leaving the employee to do their jobs. This is a mistake. The seventh and crucial step is to develop a process for regularly checking in with your employees.

Relationships are essential in business, and regularly checking in with your employees builds that relationship and increases employee retention. These relationships provide you with the following opportunities:

- Stay aware of morale
- Become aware of problems to be addressed
- Continue to emphasize the vision and mission
- Stay up to date on workloads to know when additional hires are necessary

HOW TO LET PEOPLE GO WHEN NECESSARY

By following my Seven-Step Hiring for Success Framework, you can find great candidates, hire the right people, and onboard them properly. However, despite all of our best efforts, there may come a time you realize an employee is not aligned with your vision and mission and will have to be let go.

When this happens, don't take it personally. It is not a personal failure. It happens regularly to business owners. It happened to me.

I was once stopped by someone asking if they could talk with me. Of course, I said yes, assuming they may want to talk about scheduling an appointment or a referral. Instead, she said she wanted to talk about one of my therapists.

She said she admired how hard I worked, my active marketing, and what I do in the community. She wouldn't want to see my business go down the drain because an employee acted unethically.

Obviously, I asked for details. She told me that a particular therapist had been outside drinking alcohol and dancing with a client after their session. This client had substance abuse issues, and the therapist got in the car and drove to another session after this party scene.

My next question was if she had any proof. She told me she had videoed the entire event and sent me that recording.

I called the therapist and told her not to see any more clients and that we needed to meet immediately. When we spoke, the therapist did not deny anything. She did not see anything wrong with her actions. Furthermore, she stated she had planned to pick up the client to go clubbing on her birthday.

I terminated her employment immediately, informed the licensing board, and sent the video to the licensing board.

While that was an unpleasant event, I did not take it personally. The problem did not lie with me. It was the lack of ethics on the part of that therapist. When this happens, do not put guilt on yourself. Instead, respond decisively and learn from the experience.

This work of responding decisively may come more naturally to some business owners than others. Everyone has different personalities. Confrontation can be brutal for some people. Whatever personality you have is fine, and your feelings are valid. However, there is more to consider here than your feelings.

I want to say this in the strongest possible way. In a private setting, I would not hesitate to use strong language to communicate my point. It is that important. You may not feel comfortable with confrontation, but THIS IS YOUR BUSINESS. You are obligated to the welfare of that business and your clients. You may feel uncomfortable with confrontation; do it anyway. You may feel knots in your stomach and think you might vomit; do it anyway. You may feel lightheaded and fear you will pass out; do it anyway. Your responsibility is not to feel good. It is to protect your reputation, your business, and your clients. Deal with the situation immediately and decisively, regardless of how you feel.

Then, once we are ready to act decisively, these are steps to take so you can move through the process wisely.

The first is to investigate. Business decisions are based on facts. I was fortunate in my situation that someone recorded the event and was willing to come to me with the information. You may not be that fortunate, but regardless of the effort it takes, investigate until you have the proper information to make a decision.

The second is to react decisively and professionally. Protect your business, but also work to protect other businesses and clients. In my example, I did not stop by terminating the employee. I provided all the information to the licensing board. We all have a responsibility beyond our own businesses. We have to protect our industry and clients everywhere.

The third is to learn from the situation. During this reflection and learning process, it is helpful to perform a SGOT analysis. It is not just for your business as a whole. You can do a small check-in SGOT analysis based on a particular situation. This process helps reveal what went wrong so steps can be taken to improve. These are some of the things I learned:

1. Not everyone has high ethics, and I should never assume that they do

2. Ask other questions during the interview, particularly regarding ethics

3. Make additions to my procedure manual, clearly stating my ethical standards

BUILDING A TEAM INVOLVES PLANNING, ORGANIZATION, INVESTIGATION, DETERMINATION, AND INSTINCT. BY FOLLOWING MY MULTI-MILLION-DOLLAR PRIVATE PRACTICE HIRING FRAMEWORK™, YOU CAN AVOID THE ANXIETY AND GUESSWORK AND FOLLOW A PROVEN PLAN FOR BUILDING A GREAT TEAM. YOU WERE NEVER MEANT TO BE SUPERHUMAN AND CARRY EVERY

RESPONSIBILITY YOURSELF. HIRE YOUR COACH, FOLLOW MY HIRING FOR SUCCESS FRAMEWORK, AND ACT DECISIVELY WHEN AN EMPLOYEE DOES NOT ALIGN WITH YOUR BUSINESS. BY BUILDING THE RIGHT TEAM, YOU WILL HAVE WHAT YOU NEED FOR THAT THRIVING BUSINESS OF YOUR DREAMS.

CHAPTER TAKEAWAYS

- Many business owners try to take care of everything themselves because of fear about hiring.
- Developing effective hiring processes will help ensure you have the right team to support your vision.
- Hire people before your business has a dire need for them.
- Hiring a business coach, a consultant, and a mentor can help ensure you make the right business decisions from the start.
- The right job post and screening tools can help narrow down the candidate field.
- Interviewing candidates several times helps ensure you make the right hiring decision.
- Your employee journey and onboarding process is important for employee retention.
- For long term business success it's vital to check in with your staff regularly.
- Having a strategy for letting people go when they don't work out as an employee can make the process simpler.

Chapter 16

Multi-Million-Dollar Personal Development

I remember calling my writing coach, asking her, "Do you think I am a good enough writer to write a book?" That insecure little girl that came from the Dominican Republic at the age of twelve was still inside me. I was working with my writing coach to develop my skills in blog writing and developing the educational aspect of my website. I was growing as a writer, but I wanted more. I wanted to share my story.

Since childhood, I dreamed of being an author. As an adult, I felt a need to communicate my experience of adversity and how I overcame those tough times to develop a successful private practice. I knew that my life could be an inspiration and a lesson for others facing hardship. My story could encourage, educate, and help people.

Yet part of me was still that twelve-year-old girl with all her insecurities. When I came from the Dominican Republic, I was enrolled in a bilingual education program where lessons and assignments were often in Spanish. I was living in a Spanish-speaking household. I was in a Spanish-speaking church and community. My opportunities to develop as an English speaker were limited.

Years later, as a business owner, I was full of both ambition and apprehension as I approached my writing coach with that question, "Do you think I am a good enough writer to write a book?"

Her answer took my life in a new and wonderful direction. She said, "I think you have an amazing story and the expertise to turn your story into a book people need."

I began working with her to develop my book-writing skills, and the result was my first book, *Unbreakable*. It fulfilled a dream I had had since I was seven years old. Furthermore, it was the inspiration to many that I hoped it would be. As I write this book, *Unbreakable* is receiving rave reviews from readers, and the journal is recently available. My story, my book, reached the number one spot on one category of the Amazon bestsellers list and was consistently top three in multiple categories for weeks.

One quality took me from years of insecurity to an author on the Amazon bestsellers list. That quality is my commitment to personal development.

Being a business owner is not all about business. Reaching your full potential in your professional development will largely depend on your personal growth. A personal development plan is a must if you are going to be the best version of yourself.

So, what is personal development? It is the ongoing process of improvement through acquiring new knowledge, skills, and insights. It is taking action that leads to positive changes in your life.

Keeping a mindset of continuous personal development leads to several positive impacts on your life and business, which include the following:

1. Improved Leadership Skills: Business owners must be good leaders to inspire and motivate employees. Personal development helps enhance leadership skills, increasing employee engagement, productivity, and employee retention.

2. Better Decision-Making: Critical thinking and decision-making skills are vital for running a successful business, and this comes from staying informed. Continuous learning and education are vital for making the right decisions today rather than being stuck in previous methods.

3. Enhanced Communication Skills: Effective communication is necessary for building strong relationships with clients, employees, and the public. Personal development helps improve communication skills, including listening, public speaking, writing, and networking, leading to better relationships and a wider audience for your vision and message.

4. Increased Confidence and Resilience: Owning a business is challenging. Personal development helps business owners develop the confidence and resilience to overcome obstacles and persist through tough times. Struggles become areas of growth. Hardships become an opportunity rather than a defeat.

In a rapidly changing world, wise business owners will continually develop new knowledge, skills, and insights. Having the courage to make positive changes will pay off personally and professionally, but personal growth doesn't happen by accident. It takes commitment, a vision for what you want to achieve, and a plan to get there. It will involve all of the following:

- Self-assessment
- Goal setting
- Clarifying your goals
- Developing a support system
- Celebrating your journey

SELF-ASSESSMENT

MULTI-MILLION DOLLAR PRIVATE PRACTICE SYSTEMS AND SUPPORTS FRAMEWORK™

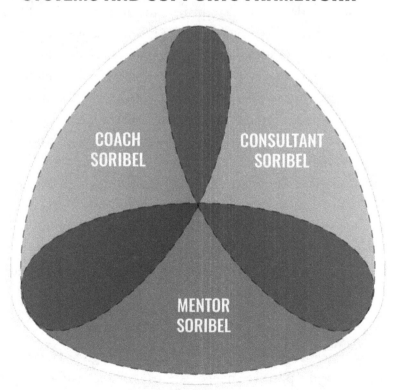

Personal development begins with self-assessment. Transformation does not happen without understanding where you are and where you want to be. Your personal development journey can only begin where you are right now, and it will lead to the place you visualize and work toward. A time of honest self-reflection is necessary to assess your current state, which is a perfect time for a SGOT analysis.

When I began my business, I meditated, visualized, and developed my vision of what I wanted to achieve. I wanted my practice to involve a strong element of education. I wanted my website to be an educational hub.

As I visualized this education hub, those insecurities about writing outside my native language were clearly my area for growth. I wanted to find a way to use my strengths to address my growth areas in writing.

My strengths include the ability to ask for help, hire help, and give up control when needed. I can trust the people I hire to guide me. These are the strengths that would lead to overcoming those insecurities. This self-assessment led me to know I needed a writing coach to address my area of growth.

However, there is an important point that you need to understand as you do this. Self-assessment does not involve comparisons. Understand this and take it to heart. This is not a time to compare yourself to other people. Family, friends, and co-workers are not part of this stage of the process.

Everybody's personal life and career development are different. Everyone has different opportunities and resources, with a different path to success. Comparisons lead to judgments, and judgments create a negative story. Thoughts such as "I'm not good enough" or "I'm not worthy" poorly affect self-esteem and make self-assessment all the more difficult.

By putting aside the comparisons, you can start your personal development plan by taking time to learn about yourself. Identify where you are now and potential growth areas in your life. Assess all areas of your life, including the following:

How satisfied are you with the current shape of your life in each area on a scale of 1–10?

- Family
- Career
- Friends
- Finances
- Physical health
- Quality of life
- Overall well-being
- Work-life balance
- Mental health

Then, evaluate how you got where you are.

- What action or inaction helped you become who you are today?

Then, imagine where you want to be.

- Where do you want your business to be?
- Your relationships?
- Your family life?
- How will you feel once you have the life you want?
- How will your thought patterns change?

All these questions lead naturally to setting goals.

GOAL-SETTING

The areas where you are least satisfied are areas of personal development. For each area of dissatisfaction, identify one thing you can do to move to the next level. These are your personal development goals.

Set your goals based on where you are at this moment of your journey. While I dreamed of being an author since childhood, that was not an immediate goal when I started my business. There were steps to take and levels to climb before I was ready to share my story. Each moment brings an opportunity for self-development.

For example, for me, college was a step. It allowed me to move to a new level in my personal growth. Working in the mental health field for other agencies was a step I needed to take. Becoming a business owner with my private practice was another level of learning.

Each new level brought discomfort and insecurity, learning, and growth. When I started my private practice, I had no idea writing would be such a big part of it. Deciding to add writing into my business plan tapped into my insecurities but also allowed me to overcome them. Each level you achieve is another measure along the journey and will naturally lead you to another professional and personal development goal, so don't try to go too fast. Let each step be one closer to your dreams.

Make your goals specific and measurable: Vague goals are difficult to achieve because it's hard to know when you've actually accomplished them. Set clear goals with specific metrics that can be tracked and measured.

Also, make your goals realistic and achievable: Set goals that challenge you but are still realistic. This is an interesting balance. Unrealistic goals can demotivate and cause you to give up before you even start. Yet, don't make them so easy that you don't have to change anything about your life to reach them. Set goals that stretch, scare, and excite you. The quest is to increase your creative capacity. Your ideal life will evolve, develop, and you will reach your full potential.

Once your goals are set, remember you don't have to attack every area at once. Trying to meet too many of your goals at once is a way of meeting none of them. Pick one or two categories where you are most dissatisfied and create self-improvement goals around those areas.

I have already mentioned my goal of creating an educational hub on my website, so that will be my focus here. Of course, I had other goals, but that was one that I saw as a crucial element to my service to the client and my marketing efforts.

The next step was to clarify these goals.

CLARIFY THE GOALS

Clarifying your goals requires the following:

- Identify your motivation: Understand why you want to achieve this goal. Identify the benefits you will gain from achieving it, who it will help, how it will advance your business, and the consequences of not achieving it.
- Break down the goal: Break down your goal into smaller, achievable steps. Instead of setting one big goal, break it down into smaller, manageable steps. This will make it easier to track progress and help you stay motivated. You may need to read about time management. You may need to learn to disconnect from electronics and be present with your children when you're home. Whatever it is, be clear and specific about what you want to achieve.

- Set deadlines: Set deadlines for each step toward your goal. This will help you stay on track and ensure that you are making progress toward your goal.
- Develop a plan: Develop a plan to achieve your goal. This should include the steps you need to take, the resources you need, and the support you require.
- Review and adjust: Regularly review your progress towards your goal and adjust your plan as needed. This will help you stay focused, adapt to changes that may impact your goal, and take advantage of new opportunities.

For my goal of creating an educational hub, I visualized an impact on the lives of the community members and even other therapists. I wanted to develop educational blogs and articles that would be available online and sent by email to clients. I saw this as an important service to clients and professionals and an important aspect of marketing. It would demonstrate who I am and what services I can provide.

I began to set my action steps and timeline. My goal would require website design and professional writing skills. I had the knowledge to provide educational materials on important topics, and I knew the support system I would need to deliver this knowledge in an excellent way. I would need a writing coach.

DEVELOP A SUPPORT SYSTEM

You have assessed your areas for improvement, set your goals, and have them clarified in your mind. It is time to get to work on your self-development goals. Now you need a cohesive system around you to support and help in your learning process.

Help can come in many forms, and you should seek out all you need. Seek help from a therapist, a life coach, self-development books, online learning, and conversations with people living a life similar to what you want. Problem-solving isn't about having all the answers. It is about the journey of finding them.

Of course, one of the best steps you can take is to hire a coach, and this does not need to be limited to one area of growth. I always hire the people I need to learn new skills.

In addition to my writing, I am working to develop my public speaking ability to become an expert-level public speaker. So, I hired a public speaking coach who is helping me develop my topics, structure speaking events, and refine my communication skills.

Therefore, as I work toward my goals, some of the resources I utilize include:

- A public speaking coach
- A writing coach
- A business coach
- Business mastermind groups
- Courses, seminars, retreats, and books

Whatever area I identify as a growth area, I will seek new methods of learning and an expert to help. A coach helps keep you in that growth mindset and push past your comfort zone, developing the self-confidence to attain your dreams.

A coach is there to walk with you, keeping you accountable and focused. It can be easy to make excuses in our minds, but sharing those excuses out loud for a coach to hear is much more difficult. That accountability is a strong motivator.

The elements we are exploring here are not only about your career path. It is a lifelong process of learning. So, in addition to hiring coaches, there are some positive personal habits to develop as you expand your self-improvement system.

- Reading for self-development. Read every day. I don't typically read a whole book. One of my mentors told me to do this: Go to the table of contents and look for parts and chapters you need. Read those chapters. It's not necessary to sit and read a whole book. Read for knowledge, understanding, and development.
- Personal development courses. These can be online or in-person.
- Networking. Find events, conferences, seminars, coaching programs, and consulting programs. These are great places to meet and learn from other professionals.

As you develop your support system, your personal development skills will be enhanced. You won't have to do it alone. You will have a cohesive system around you that will make the learning process natural and even enjoyable.

CELEBRATE YOUR JOURNEY

Milestones are important. Celebrate each one. Celebrate each time you reach a goal and clear that benchmark of self-improvement.

My goal was to create an education hub for my clients, therapists, and beyond. I wanted it to help people but also be part of my marketing, showing the values I brought to my business. When people see that website is not simply trying to sell my private practice but is actually there to help them, they see what my practice is about.

I visualized this educational hub, set it as a goal, clarified it, and developed my support. Today that goal is a reality. I continually get feedback from both clients and therapists. Therapists use the website to give homework and to help the clients between sessions.

We also use these blogs in our email marketing campaign. We email educational materials to our clients, and our opening rate on those emails is amazing. A great opening rate for an email campaign would be twenty-seven percent. My opening rate has consistently been between forty-two percent and fifty-three percent. That is phenomenal, and I am happy to celebrate it.

By following this method of personal development, I have been able to grow my private practice, create that education hub, become a keynote speaker, and also a popular author. Each one of these is something I celebrate, and it propels me to my next self-assessment and set of goals. It doesn't stop.

Now, that insecure little girl that immigrated from the Dominican Republic is pursuing a Doctorate in Social Work at Walden University. My professors regularly compliment my writing, and I receive their praise with joy. It validates all the hard work I have put in and the support I put around me. Writing began as an area of growth for me. Yet I had important goals to pursue. Now I have reached great heights in writing as both an author and a doctoral student.

It all comes through a dedication to personal development. I didn't give up because it was outside my current area of genius. I found the support and training I needed, hired the right help, worked hard, and developed the necessary skills. This is what leads to celebration.

Celebrating milestones can boost self-confidence, provide motivation to continue the journey, and inspire others to embark on their own personal development journeys.

So find ways to celebrate the achievement of each of your goals. It can be in various ways, such as treating yourself to something special, sharing the accomplishment with friends and family, or hosting a small gathering.

When you have set a goal, clarified it, gathered your support, and worked toward your goal, you are improving as a person and as a business owner. Personal development is your method of reaching your greatest potential and living out your dreams. When you reach that next great height, take a little time to celebrate.

Other aspects of your business: Work with an attorney to ensure you're meeting all legal expectations and create policies for hiring and onboarding.

As my business and purpose have expanded, I've added writing staff and a website designer, and partnered with many others to make my brand and dream as strong as possible. That isn't to say the people I hire or bring on board always work out. Sometimes people don't fit in with the mission and values of your business. Don't spend too much time worrying about that. The people who are meant to be part of your journey will stay. God will take care of the rest.

CHAPTER TAKEAWAYS

- Reaching your full potential requires constant personal growth.
- You must work to improve leadership skills, communication, decision-making, and resilience.
- You can use the SGOT analysis as a means of assessing yourself as well as your business.
- Your life-satisfaction is important and will reflect in your business.
- A self-analysis can lead to goal setting for personal growth.
- Finding support for your personal development goals is the best way to ensure you meet them.
- Celebrating personal achievements and reflecting on how far you've come can increase motivation.

Chapter 17

Multi-Million-Dollar Private Practice Systems and Supports Framework™

"You do not rise to the level of your goals.
You fall to the level of your systems."
James Clear, Atomic Habits

I like this quote from James Clear, but I'd take it a step further. Your success depends not on your effort, not on your goals, but instead on a combination of systems and supports. Let me explain.

I woke up one Monday morning in April with a headache, body aches, and all the telltale signs that my body was fighting an infection. My assistant, Eneercida, was visiting from the Dominican Republic because this was the week of my book launch for

Unbreakable. We had a tight schedule this week of all the things we needed to do to be ready for the event, and my body was revolting.

As a private practice owner, you need to think of yourself as someone who runs a business. Hopefully, by the time you've reached this chapter, your mindset has shifted and you're ready to embrace the entrepreneurial spirit. But, I must caution you.

No matter how big your goals are, no matter how much you plan, no matter how much energy and effort you put into your business, you will not succeed without systems and support.

If I didn't have systems in place to run my private practice without my intervention. I wouldn't be able to give in to my body's need for rest when I'm sick. I would have to drag myself to my desk despite an achy head and fever to ensure that billing was done, that credentialing paperwork was in order, and that new clients had a seamless start to their experience. If I had to do that, I'd be too wrung out to attend my book launch and celebrate with all the supporters who made it possible. I wouldn't be able to deliver my planned speech because I would have a sore throat and my body would crave sleep.

Because of my systems, my business can operate when I'm not available. Whether I'm vacationing in Dubai, sleeping off a cold, or grieving a loss, I am confident I can step away, do what I need to do to care for myself, and come back to a profitable, impactful business.

Because of the supports I have set up, I know that things are taken care of in my absence. I can trust my party planner to get the book launch ready. I trust my assistant to keep my social media up to date, and I trust my writing coach and business coach to support me, remain flexible when I need a break, and help me to absolutely rock this entrepreneur thing when I'm back to myself.

I want the same for you. So let's dive into the systems and supports you will need as you start and scale your private practice.

To begin, you need to identify your area of genius. What work do you do best? Where do your skills shine?

My most impactful skills involve business management and coaching others in overcoming obstacles and building their dreams. So, anything outside of that is something I design systems for, hire support for, or both.

The mindset of many mental health and healthcare providers is that they have to do everything themselves, they have to have control of how everything is done and when it gets done. If that's your mindset, then we need to start there.

MINDSET SHIFT—ACCEPT SUPPORT, CREATE SYSTEMS

As a young child, I saw all the women around me running households, caring for children, and doting on husbands who may or may not have deserved their attention. As a young Dominican woman, I was trained to behave similarly. I learned how to be a "good wife and mother" at a young age. My mother and aunts tried to instill their values in me. But there was a problem with that. I dreamed of owning my own business, and creating a massive impact in the world. My dreams could not be contained by a kitchen or a tidy home; they stretched further. My dreams were illustrative of my values. I valued entrepreneurship. I valued motherhood, and wanted to be a mother, but I did not want to be a stay-at-home mom. So, I decided at a young age that anything I didn't like doing, and anything that didn't align with my values wasn't worth doing long-term. Does that mean I don't know how to cook or do laundry? Of course not.

I learn how to do anything I need to do to run my house and business in case I need to step in and get it done. But, if I can, I outsource it to someone who loves and values that work as part of their personal mission.

Let's connect this concept to business decisions. If my time is worth one hundred dollars per hour, and it takes me a whole working day to clean the house, that's the same as investing $800. But if I pay someone to do it at twenty-five or fifty dollars per hour, or even at one hundred dollars, and they do it faster, it's a better business decision to let them do it. Building a way for other people to work in their area of genius gives me more time to make a bigger impact and allows them to make money to support their lives.

In business, I know how to do credentialing and billing to insurance companies. I choose not to because it doesn't make financial sense to do so. It makes more sense to spend time in my area of genius and pay someone else who excels in credentialing to work that part of the business. How much is your time worth in your business? What is your area of genius? What can you outsource so you can maximize the time you spend in your area of genius?

Building a team that includes support for every area that is outside your genius will yield the following benefits.

- You'll build a solid foundation for your business so it's able to adapt to changing markets and problems that arise.
- Your solid foundation will allow you to scale and grow faster because your systems will take care of the incoming work.
- You give other people the opportunity to showcase their talents and abilities.
- You'll increase your impact on the world.

As a business owner, you get to decide the shape of your life. You get to decide how much time you spend strategizing, networking, meeting with clients, and on vacation. Do you want to continue working on every part of your business? Do you want to continue to feel burned out and exhausted?

Make the decision today to get out of this dirty chair, the one that tells you a business owner must do everything themselves if they want it done right. Let's write a different story that says:

"I deserve to work in my area of genius because that's where I have the greatest impact on the world. I invite in the support I need to build a solid foundation, develop systems, and scale my business to maximize both profit and impact."

Now that you have a new story, let's get down to the business of setting up systems and supports.

SYSTEMS AND SUPPORTS FOR A SOLID FOUNDATION

Your systems are like your standard operating procedures. These include your employee experience and your client experience paths. You may consider the following systems to help your business run itself so you can go on vacation. I'm not kidding—setting up the right systems ensures your business can run without you.

To begin, think about the client's journey. From the moment a potential client finds one of your therapists on *Psychology Today*, or a Google search, what is the experience you want the client to have?

How do you want the client to feel about that experience?
How will they schedule appointments or a consultation?
How will insurance billing work in your practice?
What about emails for education and reminders?
Will clients meet in your office or via telehealth?
What support do you need for each part of your client journey?

You'll need to consider finding services for the following:
- Phone service
- Email service
- Billing service
- Appointment scheduling
- Cancellation policies
- Insurance credentialing
- Internet service
- Telehealth platform that guarantees privacy

The more effort you put into building a seamless client journey that matches them with the best possible services, the more likely you are to retain them long term and earn referrals for their friends and family.

Next, you'll want to lay out your employee journey. How do you want your company to interact with employees and independent contractors? Start with your application process, think through onboarding, and don't forget to consider long-term relationship building.

The systems you'll want to set up for an employee journey include a recruiter or other way to find qualified candidates, a human resource platform, operational documents including standard operating procedures and standards for your private practice, a payroll system, email system, telehealth portal, comfortable office space, and an electronic health record system that is user-friendly and trustworthy.

For ongoing support and development, consider systems for training, and regular check-ins with staff to ensure they are satisfied with the work they do. The more satisfied your employees are, the longer you'll retain them, and the harder they'll work for you.

Setting up your employee journey is something you should do before you hire anyone. You can always make changes as you hire and find out that parts of your system aren't working. It's easy to change a flawed plan, but it's impossible to change a plan that never existed.

You're investing in a seamless client journey and a supportive employee journey, but that's not enough. Your business exists to serve clients and support your employees in reaching their goals, but your business should also work for you. That's why hiring support for you as a business owner is one of the most important ways to invest in your business.

The most impactful support you can hire for yourself and your business is a coach. A study published in Gender in Management evaluated how coaching programs affected the self-efficacy of female entrepreneurs. Self-efficacy is your belief that you can accomplish what you set out to do in your life and business. The study found that female entrepreneurs benefited from a business coaching program, especially during the start-up phase. Coaching increased their ability to learn new skills, influence others, and increased energy and motivation.[4]

I've found this to be true in my business. I hired a coach and mentor right away. In fact, early in my entrepreneurial journey, when I was still working in schools and starting my private practice part time, all my early earnings went right to my coach. Doing this increased my confidence, gave me the support I needed for decision-making, and ensured that I didn't miss any crucial steps in building the foundation of my business.

---

4   Hunt, C.M., Fielden, S. and Woolnough, H.M. (2019), "The potential of online coaching to develop female entrepreneurial self-efficacy," *Gender in Management*, Vol. 34 No. 8, pp. 685–701. https://doi.org/10.1108/GM-02-2019-0021

When I'm working with new private practice owners, I recommend they hire three people for personal support in their entrepreneurial journey. Sometimes, if you're lucky, you can find all three of these supports in one person. Let me explain.

The first person you need to hire is a coach. A coach will focus primarily on asking the right questions and guiding you to come up with your own answers. Coaches are excellent at mindset work and helping you reframe your limiting beliefs. Mindset is ninety to ninety-five percent of your business success, which is why I recommend starting with a coach.

You'll also need a consultant. A consultant is someone who knows how to start, run, and scale a business. They may do a bit of coaching but will also jump in to help you make decisions when you feel stuck. Coaching is great, but sometimes you can't come up with the answers on your own and need someone who will tell you whether you need to hire a copywriter or a social media specialist next.

A mentor is someone who has done exactly what you want to do. If you're starting a group practice on a private pay model, you'll want someone who has that experience. If you're starting a solo practice taking insurance reimbursement rates, you'll want a mentor who has done that. Mentors guide with experience.

I cannot emphasize enough the importance of hiring someone who knows the business you're in. If you were a tomato farmer, you wouldn't hire a coach or consultant who only has experience growing mangoes. While they may have general farming knowledge, they can't tell you how to successfully run a tomato farm— the methods are different. If you're a mental health practitioner starting or scaling a private practice, you need to hire people well-versed in mental health private practice.

Now, let's say you're a business owner starting a solo practice, with dreams of running a group practice operating as both insurance pay and private pay. Maybe you even want to add public speaker or social media influencer to your resume. If you find a business coach and consultant who has run a solo practice, transitioned to a successful group practice model, and found other ways to increase revenue beyond just offering one-on-one therapy sessions, then you've found all three in one person. Grab ahold of them, and get ready for incredible profit and impact.

CHAPTER TAKEAWAYS

- Having systems in place for your daily operations will ensure your business can run even if you need a vacation or a sick day.
- No one can build a legacy alone; you need to accept support.
- Mapping out your client's journey can help you develop systems and find the right support to ensure smooth business operation.
- You must also have systems in place for your employee journey including onboarding, and standard operating procedures.
- A business coach, mentor, and consultant is the most vital support for any business owner.

Conclusion and Next Steps

I designed this book as a guide—or maybe *curriculum* is a better word—for private practice owners who want to build a profitable, impactful business without burning themselves out. There are two pieces of advice I hope you get from reading this book.

1. You cannot build your business in isolation. A legacy-making business requires support.
2. You must align your purpose, vision, and mission and ensure every decision you make is also in alignment.

You will need the support of your family and friends. Sometimes, well-meaning loved ones will caution you against starting your business, or making moves to grow it. In that case, you may need to expand your circle to find those who support your dreams.

You will need the support of hired staff to help manage billing, credentialing, accounting, and more. Trying to do everything will take you away from your genius.

You need support from someone who has built the sort of business you want to create. You need someone to encourage, to push, and to ask the right questions. Hiring this support is the best possible investment in the success of your private practice.

Aligning your purpose, vision and mission will ensure that you are doing the work you're meant to do in this world. Alignment will energize you, support your decision-making, and help you create the impact you want to have on the world.

If you're ready to create your Multi-Million-Dollar Private Practice, I have the resources and programs you need. I invite you to take the next steps, outlined below. Follow the associated link or QR code for each step to learn more and get started today.

Email me and tell me about your biggest takeaway from this book, and the area you're struggling with most as you build your private practice at soribel@soribelmartinez.com or use the QR code below

Email Soribel

Download my Multi-Million Dollar Business Finance E-book. Every business owner needs sound financial advice to build and scale to over a million dollars in revenue. This e-book is the private practice owner's essential guide to running the financial side of their business.

Multi-Million Dollar Business Finance E-book

Take the Million-Dollar Private Practice Quiz to help evaluate where you are in your business now, and what your next steps are.

Million-Dollar Private Practice Quiz

Join my free Facebook community to collaborate with like-minded professionals building their purpose-driven private practice. In addition to community, you'll get tips from me and insight into how you can make the Multi-Million-Dollar Private Practice Framework ™ work for you and your business.

Million-Dollar Private Practice Facebook Community

Enroll in the Multi-Million-Dollar Private Practice Online Course. This course takes you through each of the eight pillars of my Multi-Million-Dollar Private Practice Framework™ in a self-paced course. Combined with this book, and the Facebook community you'll get all the tools you need to build and scale your practice.

Multi-Million-Dollar Private Practice Online Course

Schedule your business assessment. I offer three levels of assessment depending on where you are in your business-building journey.

The Multi-Million-Dollar Business Mindset Assessment: a one-on-one session with me and a detailed plan to address any mindset issues holding you back from creating the life and business of your dreams.

Book Your Mindset Assessment

The Multi-Million-Dollar Marketing Plan Assessment: Marketing is the most difficult part of business for many people I work with. This assessment will help you figure out what's stopping you from marketing your practice effectively and give you detailed feedback on the best marketing strategies to help you build a profitable, impactful business.

Book Your Marketing Assessment

The Multi-Million-Dollar Business Analysis Assessment: for private practice owners who are ready to assess every area of their business from legal structures to goal setting, and even marketing. This assessment includes both the mindset and marketing pieces and then challenges you to dive deeper into your goal setting, personal development, and team building practices to identify growth areas and opportunities.

Book Your Business Analysis Assessment

Sign up for the Multi-Million-Dollar Private Practice Group Coaching Program. This is a four-month program that grants you access to the Multi-Million-Dollar Private Practice Manual, and all of my expertise as well as a network of like-minded mental health professionals.

Multi-Million-Dollar Private Practice Group Coaching Program

If you are a solo provider and want more personalized one-to-one support as you transition to group practice, then my personalized Million-Dollar Private Practice Year-Long Coaching Program is for you. You'll get one on one sessions with me, guidance with every step of business startup and growth, and all the tools in my Multi-Million-Dollar Private Practice Manual.

Million-Dollar Private Practice Year-Long Coaching Program

If you are a group practice owner focused on scaling your practice and increasing profit and revenue, my exclusive, one-on-one Million-Dollar Private Practice Year-Long Mentorship Program is for you. A step up from my coaching program, the mentorship comes with everything in my coaching program as well as on-demand access to me and my expertise at every stage of business growth.

Million-Dollar Private Practice Year-Long Mentorship Program

JC's Precious Minds Foundation

JC's Precious Minds Foundation seeks to help single mothers of children with disabilities with financial and educational resources. Soribel began the foundation to honor the memory of her son, Jean-Carlos who was stillborn at thirty-six weeks. Grief is like the ocean, with small waves that cause you to catch your breath, and large waves that threaten to knock you over. The ocean is powerful, and so is grief. If you channel it, you can use it to create a greater impact in the world than you dreamed possible.

JC's Precious Minds Foundation provides financial resources, housing, food, clothing, special education, testing services, occupational, physical, and speech therapy, psychological services, and extracurricular activities to special needs children of single mothers in the Dominican Republic. In addition to helping children reach their potential, the foundation assists single mothers with returning to school or/and starting their own business. Every child, and every woman deserves the support necessary to thrive.

In December 2022 the foundation received its first donation of $150,000. The foundation began with four families and currently serves ten with plans to further expand.

To learn more, visit our website here. https://jcpreciousmind-foundation.org/

JC'S PRECIOUS MIND FOUNDATION RECIPIENT

"First and foremost, we want to express our gratitude to this wonderful initiative, JC's Precious Mind Foundation, which has impacted the lives of every member of this family.

I experienced a sense of the end of the world when Ramses was diagnosed with autism. With him, it was nearly impossible to leave the house because I was so worried about his future that I sobbed nonstop for a while. Then, in 2021, I obtained assistance from JC's Precious Mind Foundation, who were like angels sent by God. Since that time, my family's dynamic has totally changed.

Since Ramses began taking classes, receiving therapy, and receiving food, we have been able to witness his progress to the extent that our son Ramses is no longer the same as he was a year ago. We are moved by every new word he says, every new food he requests and tries, and by every new action he takes. Everything I once imagined my son could do, he has accomplished thanks to the collaboration and support of JC's Precious Mind Foundation. We can only say THANK YOU because without your assistance, who knows where we would be."

—**Mercedes Alejandrina Tavarez,** mother of Ramsés, a six-year-old boy

About the Author

As a Business Coach and Consultant, Soribel designs strategies for optimal business growth. Soribel is a purpose-driven entrepreneur who strives to help others create the lives of their dreams. She helps private practice owners build and scale their businesses using The Multi-Million-Dollar Private Practice Framework™.

Soribel is a Licensed Clinical Psychotherapist, with over twenty-five years of experience, and a track record of helping people overcome obstacles and create the life they want. She developed the Multi-Million-Dollar Private Practice Framework™ to build and scale SMPsychotherapy and Counseling Services into the dynamic practice it is today. SMPsychotherapy employs over twenty-five licensed mental health therapists, two psychiatric mental health nurse practitioners, and administrative staff. The thriving group practice serves over eleven thousand clients.

Soribel expanded her purpose to help women build their dreams by founding JC's Precious Minds Foundation in 2021 to honor the memory of her son, Jean-Carlos. Soribel believes in honoring the women and family members who came before her and paved the path to her success. She believes in honoring herself by answering the call for her purpose, and she seeks to honor the future generation by creating a legacy and a blueprint for growth and success.

In addition to being a business coach, CEO, and the founder of a non-profit, Soribel is a mother, a speaker, a storyteller, an adjunct professor of Psychology at Post University, a member of the Post University's Malcolm Baldrige School of Business-Management Advisory Board. She's a bestselling author and a concierge sex therapist. Soribel lives in Connecticut with her mother and son, John Anthony. She spends her free time with family, traveling around the world, reading, and learning as much as she can.

A free ebook edition is available with the purchase of this book.

To claim your free ebook edition:

1. Visit MorganJamesBOGO.com
2. Sign your name CLEARLY in the space
3. Complete the form and submit a photo of the entire copyright page
4. You or your friend can download the ebook to your preferred device

Morgan James BOGO™

A **FREE** ebook edition is available for you or a friend with the purchase of this print book.

CLEARLY SIGN YOUR NAME ABOVE

Instructions to claim your free ebook edition:
1. Visit MorganJamesBOGO.com
2. Sign your name CLEARLY in the space above
3. Complete the form and submit a photo of this entire page
4. You or your friend can download the ebook to your preferred device

Print & Digital Together Forever.

Snap a photo

Free ebook

Read anywhere

Printed in the USA
CPSIA information can be obtained
at www.ICGtesting.com
JSHW082107120424
61084JS00002B/44